# A Map
# of Love

Around Wales With Dylan Thomas

Jackie Hayden

Jackie Hayden has to date published ten books, the latest of which is *My Boy*, the story of the late Irish rock star Philip Lynott of Thin Lizzy which he wrote based on 100 hours of interviews with Lynott's mother Philomena. The book spent six weeks at number one on the Irish non-fiction charts in 2011.

Hayden's day job is as Contributing Editor for *Hot Press*, Ireland's premier rock music magazine. Over the years he has interviewed a diverse range of subjects, including Bob Geldof, The Corrs, Sinead O'Connor, American composer Steve Reich, comedian Jackie Mason, the Irish president Michael D Higgins, politicians David Norris and Gay Mitchell, and Sinn Féin leader Gerry Adams.

In a previous life as Marketing Manager with Sony Ireland he signed U2 to their first record contract in 1979. He was invited by the Irish president Michael D Higgins to serve on a government Task Force to explore ways in which government could assist Irish musicians, and was appointed Chairman of a government committee to examine the International Marketing of Irish Music. He has lectured on the music industry at seminars, colleges and universities all over Ireland and in Wales, Spain, Germany, France and the USA, and is regularly interviewed on Irish and British radio about developments in the music scene. He has also edited the books *From The Cradle To The Stage* by Alan Swan, and *Hidden Grief* by Vanessa Grattan.

Published by:
Iconau in collaboration with Fflach

Glan Morfa       Llys-y-Coed
Ferryside         Cardigan
SA17 5TF       SA43 3AH
www.iconau.com    www.fflach.co.uk

First published in 2012
© Jackie Hayden
Photographs © Wyn Jones
All rights reserved

ISBN 978-1-907476-04-4

Edited by Lucy Llewellyn

Cover design by the undercard.com
Original photograph by David Daly
Typeset in Bell MT by Lucy Llewellyn
Factual accuracy checked by Chris Ozzard
Printed and bound by Gwasg Gomer

British Library Cataloguing in Publication data

A cataloguing record for this book is available from the British Library.

# Contents

# Dylan, Dylan and Me

## An Introduction

Some people write of what they know. I write out of a sense of curiosity, to expand my own knowledge and to engage with the lives and thoughts of others whose experience might be far different from mine. In writing the text for this book and the script for the accompanying CD, I don't wish to put myself forward as a Dylan Thomas expert, nor as an academic of any kind. I regard myself as an avid reader and an enthusiastic listener who has taken enormous nourishment from Dylan's writings over the past four decades. I've been equally fascinated by his dedication to his muse, alongside his refusal to let the demands of life get in the way of enjoying himself as well as the pleasures that life and fame offered.

Working on this project with the inestimable Jim Parc Nest, as well as Richard and Wyn Jones of Fflach Records in Cardigan, presented me with several opportunities to engage more deeply with the life and character of Dylan Thomas. It enabled me to revisit his remarkable works and the main places in Wales associated with him, and in which he found so much inspiration. It may seem trite to say so, but writers do not write in a vacuum, immune from their environment or from those who people it. In that regard, Dylan's various works contain countless echoes of Wales and the Welsh.

I first discovered Dylan's poetry several decades ago when I read that the singer and songwriter Bob Dylan, already a musical hero of mine, had changed his surname from Zimmerman because of his admiration for the Welsh bard. Despite the lack of veracity of that tale, I recognised similarities between the works of both Dylans: not least in their love of words, their joy in the sound of language, and their tendency to give the full value to virtually every word they used. I also admired, and was inspired by, their refusal to obey the conventions of society or to conform meekly to the demands of their chosen fields of operation and the self-appointed high priests thereof. That Bob had clearly been inspired by folk music and musicians from this side of the Atlantic, and that Thomas was a fellow Celt, gave me an added connection to them. Yet despite that connection, both also came from cultures different from mine. While we in Ireland had been saturated by American music, film and literature for decades, Wales, despite its geographical proximity, was unexplored territory with its own language, and that difference was another attraction to me. Yes, we are fellow Celts, but we are also quite different in many of our attitudes and preoccupations, and I'm sure that that difference gave me a view of Dylan and his work that might not tally with the way he is viewed by some Welsh readers. So I set off on an adventure, one that took me to Wales many times over the following decades, and one that is still very much ongoing.

Indeed, I can remember my first visit, one that included Swansea, Laugharne and New Quay, and staying in inexpensive bed and breakfast accommodation as I made my way around. On several occasions when I mentioned, boasted even, about the reasons for my visit, I was somewhat disappointed not to be greeted with considerable appreciation by my guests. It was later suggested to me that I might have been talking to people who came from what was described as 'the chapel' areas of Wales and who did not at all approve of a man who spent so much of his time and money in pubs, possibly even neglecting his wife and children. But others have disputed that suggestion. It's equally possible that they were not as familiar with Dylan as I assumed, just as some guest house owners in Ireland might lack in appreciation for our great writers such as James Joyce or Samuel Beckett.

By and by, the Welsh Dylan's writings taught me that poetry has a value that often transcends mere meaning. I discovered that seeking meaning as a primary consideration in poetry can be as pointless as looking at the beautiful panoramic vista of the estuary at Laugharne and then casually reducing it with a negative 'ah, but, what does it mean?' I learned that a poem has a concrete existence that is not dependent on it being deconstructed and translated into something else: a simplified, watered down version of true self.

And it was through reading and hearing his evocative poems, captivating stories, the magic of *Under Milk Wood* and my engagement with Dylan's life, I came to know Wales, especially Swansea, Laugharne, New Quay, Carmarthen, Fishguard, St David's, Cardigan and beyond. While some literary purists espouse the notion that the writer's life should not concern the reader at all, and that the work should be left to stand completely alone, I've actually gained enormous pleasure from Dylan's works by visiting the places that nourished him and inspired him. Indeed, his works and his stature appeared to grow in substance the deeper I steeped myself in the places of their creation, as if they'd emerged from the very locations themselves.

The voice of Dylan, his stories and the sound of his poems all resonate with the Wales he knew, its sights, sounds, culture, mythology and religious preoccupations, its garrulous conversation, reverence for the spoken word, love of argument and political debate, as well as the foibles of the people he observed and whose company he loved to share. All of this resonates with me, perhaps especially as an Irishman, as a similar attitude can be found among the Irish. We've even invented the word 'craic' (pronounced 'crack') to cover those special social occasions when we mix conversation and argument, jokes and banter, food and drink, and maybe some music and poetry too. I was intrigued only a few years ago to see advertisements encouraging people to visit Cardiff 'for the craic'.

To me there's no doubting Dylan's Welshness. He inherited the Welsh love of oratory and the music of words, and in his *Reminiscences of Childhood* he referred to Wales with 'its wild names like peals of bells in darkness'. The Maesteg writer and biographer John Ackerman described him as 'one of us', and he referred to himself unambiguously when he said, 'One: I am a Welshman', before going on to enumerate his other key traits. The biographer George Tremlett wrote 'He loved a wider world, but the prism through which he observed it was Wales'.

Despite spending some time abroad, Dylan composed most of his poems in various parts of Wales, sometimes beginning a poem in one place and completing it in another. While he was away, he was often homesick for his native land, and in his BBC radio talk *Living In Wales* he spoke of being on a train journey through England while admitting he wanted to be in Wales.

Irish writers have often taken a different tack, especially in the middle decades of the last century, some choosing to emigrate to escape the stifling conservative conventions of Irish society fostered on part by the dominance of the Catholic Church. James Joyce, Samuel Beckett and Sean O'Casey all left Ireland and seemed to have little desire to return. Dylan did not feel that way about Wales, where he willingly spent most of his life.

It's impossible for me now to read or hear *Under Milk Wood* without thinking of the layout and environs of New Quay or Laugharne, or even of Fishguard, where it was famously filmed. In the same way, it's become virtually unimaginable for me to visit any of those places without sensing his work in the very air. There is a delightful quirkiness and a convention-defying eccentricity to the vivid characters and places in Dylan's prose works, especially *Under Milk Wood*. That appeals to my Irish nature and draws me to Wales time and time again.

Indeed, one of the most exhilarating moments of my life came when I was sitting on a public bench along the path that links the Boathouse with Brown's Hotel in Laugharne, gazing across the estuary. I was reading the poem 'Over Sir John's hill'; the hill itself rearing up on my right, a hawk magically hovering nearby while I read the lines 'he pulls to his claws and gallows, up the rays of his eyes the small birds of the bay ...' It was an indescribable moment, indelibly imprinted on my memory.

I have also been privileged to meet Dylan's daughter Aeronwy when, only a couple of years before she passed away, she gave moving readings of both her own and her father's poems at a special event at the marvellous Rhos-y-Gilwen venue built and owned by Glen Peters just outside Cardigan. Her memoir *My Father's Places* looks back with a loving but honest fondness to their times together, and among my prized possessions is a copy of the first Dylan Thomas book I ever read, *Miscellany One*, which Aeronwy kindly signed for me on that occasion. It's sitting in my workspace at home as I write this, alongside another personal favourite, number eight out of twelve copies of a special edition of 'Fern Hill' printed on Wookey Hole handmade paper, and generously given to me by Myles Pepper of the West Wales Art Centre in Fishguard.

So it was a momentous privilege for me to be present at the recording of the CD that accompanies this book in the very room at 5 Cwmdonkin Drive where Dylan was born. At times, I must admit, it was hard not to feel it was really just a film set recreation of the original house. But its current owners (coincidentally Geoff and Annie Haden, very close to my own family name) have made such efforts to ensure its authenticity that it takes little effort to imagine the Thomas family going about their daily business in its various rooms. You almost expect one or other of them to walk through the door and bid you the time of day.

To walk on what's almost become hallowed ground for Thomas admirers brought me back through all I'd read about Dylan's upbringing in that house. When I first stood on the pavement outside, maybe thirty-five years ago on my first Dylan Thomas 'pilgrimage' to Wales, I couldn't have imagined then that I'd one day work on this project with such marvellous people *inside* that house.

I was also delighted to hear that the Swansea authorities had been awarded a Development grant from the Heritage Lottery Fund to develop the nearby Cwmdonkin Park, and that there are plans to highlight its links with Dylan in a way that will encourage and inform visitors. Any and all such efforts are to be applauded, especially if they bring more people into closer contact with the poet's marvellous creations.

Those works repay revisits. They are an essential part of what draws me to Wales time and time again.

I was spurred towards this project by the wish that there had been something like it when I first discovered Dylan's country. I hope it will encourage those so inclined to move closer to this great writer, by spending time in the places that inspired him and following this map of love around Wales.

Jackie Hayden

# A Map
# of Love

# To Begin at the Beginning: Swansea The Ugly, Lovely Town

While staying in Hampshire in England, Dylan Marlais Thomas wrote, in a letter to his friend Charles Fisher, that 'Swansea is still the best place' and he also remarked 'never was there such a town'. His radio broadcast *Reminiscences of Childhood* is a tender look-back on his younger days in Swansea, although bombing during the war makes much of modern Swansea look vastly different from the town it was then.

In many ways Swansea's not hugely dissimilar from my own native Dublin, which is also a busy port and, at least in its pre-Celtic Tiger decades, had a friendly and relaxed working class feel to most of it. But I was already familiar with Swansea before I visited it for the first time, mainly from my interest in football. I was, in fact, a distant fan of Swansea Town, as the team was then known. Why a teenager in Dublin might forego adopting Liverpool or Manchester

United or Arsenal or Tottenham Hotspur as his favourite English League team might merit some explaining.

It began with a Welsh international rugby player Haydn Morgan whose name I would have come across as a fairly wide-ranging sports fan. His first name gave me the notion that I might be Welsh. Perhaps my low personal self-esteem led me to want to emphasise some difference that would set me apart from my school pals and neighbours. The thought of being Welsh through some long-forgotten, probably imaginary, ancestor had a sense of the exotic about it. In an era when few people had cars and rarely travelled or holidayed abroad, Wales fitted the bill, apparently. So when it came to choosing a favourite football team it seemed natural to pick a Welsh one and I chose Swansea (sorry, Cardiff!), a strange decision since I could not to afford to see them play, and there was little football on the telly then (we had no telly anyway). So I followed their (mis)fortunes through the newspapers, BBC sports reports and *Charles Buchan's Football Monthly* magazine.

So, on my first visit to the town I was delighted to find that the guest house I had booked was close to the Vetch Field, then the legendary home ground of my favourite team. I remember gazing in awe at the site, but, sadly, my visit took place outside the football season, so I was not able to attend a match there. But I can still remember the names of famous Welsh footballers from that era, including John and Mel Charles, Ivor and Len Allchurch, Terry Medwin, Cliff Jones ... magical names that appeared on the chewing-gum wrappers we used to collect at school in Dublin.

Soon after, my Swansea allegiance had changed from football to literature anyway. Before Dylan was born, his parents DJ, known as Jack, and Florence had moved from nearby Carmarthenshire to Sketty, an outlying suburb of Swansea, as part of a general migration from the countryside into the cities, mostly for economic and employment reasons in a markedly changing world. Swansea had latterly become a busy port, moving vast amounts of coal, steel, cement and other industrial products, and it had developed a substantial professional class too. By the time Dylan's older sister Nancy was born DJ and Florence were living in Montpellier Street, in the centre of the town, but they were in 5 Cwmdonkin Drive before her brother arrived.

Dylan was born shortly before midnight on October 27, 1914, upstairs in the front room of the house which is situated on a steep incline in the Uplands area. In this solid, semi-detached four-bedroom house he spent his happy, formative years with DJ, Florence and Nancy. Having since had the privilege of seeing inside the house it seems that DJ's salary enabled them to have a more comfortable home than I had in my own more modest working-class upbringing in the countryside outside Dublin city, and in reading the various biographies about Dylan I find little sign of poverty or real hardship.

The name Dylan came from the character Dylan Eil Ton in the mythical Welsh drama the *Mabinogion*. It can be translated as 'sea son of the wave', and in the myth he swam off and became part of the sea, suggesting to some fanciful souls that our Dylan's love of Welsh sea towns and villages might have been pre-ordained. Dylan himself, perhaps mischievously, suggested his name meant 'prince of darkness'. His second name Marlais was taken from his great-uncle who was also a poet. Furthermore, the Afon Marlais is a tributary of the River Towy in Carmarthenshire, so both his names had clear connections with water, another sign, perhaps, for a man who was to choose to live most of his life by the sea?

Dylan's doting mother, known to friends and family as Florrie, was an inveterate chatterer and a house-proud woman who often liked to employ a housemaid. She defiantly maintained her non-conformist religious attachments that came to her from her roots in Carmarthenshire, but she was not much interested in reading. She spoke Welsh, but due to her husband's indifference to the language, not much Welsh was spoken in the Thomas house. She pampered Dylan, who was a somewhat delicate child with deceptively angelic features, and she was inclined, both then and later, to turn a motherly blind eye to his weaknesses and wayward behaviour. He, in turn, was only too happy to accept her attentive coddling. In his teens, Dylan described her as 'stout, safe, confident, buried in her errands.'

In contrast, Dylan's father DJ, known as Jack, was a learned man who could be somewhat severe. He was thirty-eigt years old when Dylan was born. He had earlier won a scholarship to the University of Aberystwyth, and was now earning his living as a teacher in Swansea. He almost certainly felt disappointed and unfulfilled in his career, convinced that his talents deserved a better position in academia than that of a mere schoolmaster. In religious terms he was agnostic, possible even an Atheist. Not a very demonstrative man either, he wasn't naturally inclined to hold or hug his children. He was regarded as a fearsome figure by his pupils, and a distant man by most of his colleagues. But he read the leading literary magazines of the day and had a great lifelong reverence for literature, especially that of the Bible, Shakespeare, Lamb, Dickens, the Brontës, Coleridge, Thomas Hardy and Matthew Arnold, among others, and he passed that love to his son. His book-lined study also contained plaster statues of the great Greeks. Perhaps determined to see Dylan achieve the literary heights he himself had striven for but sadly failed to reach, he encouraged Dylan to read widely from an early age and Dylan grew to become immensely proud of his dad.

The love of books in the Thomas household echoed my own upbringing. My mother had encouraged me to read from an early age. She herself had been introduced to the pleasures of books when her own mother gave her a copy of Dickens' *Great Expectations*, so she gave me the same book. I also remember reading *Black Beauty*, Billy Bunter, Biggles, and countless other books borrowed from the public library that was conveniently located just the far side of a field our house. I have lived in only three houses since

7

leaving my parents' home, and each of those houses has been full of books. Some of them remain unread, yet their presence brings me a comfort and a reassurance that I can't quite explain.

Anthony Powell wrote a fine novel called *Books Do Furnish a Room*. Indeed they do. But books also furnish a mind and nourish the soul. I cannot imagine a life without books. Whenever I meet another avid reader I feel I need know nothing more about them to feel a kinship. I can never destroy a book, and even when I've decided l no longer need to keep a particular one, I prefer to pass it on to another reader. Nor am I phased by the arrival of the e-book. My primary focus is always on the writing, so it matters little whether I'm reading the material on paper, on a computer screen, a mobile phone or an e-reader. However I'm fascinated by the controversy stirred up by the arrival of the e-reader, with its opponents protesting about the sacrilege of reading other than on paper. I encouraged me to imagine a similar controversy around the invention of printing, with people bemoaning the fact that we would no longer be able to read handwritten scripts on parchment and all those scribes out of work so that we could all read books that would like identical. Needless to say, I have a reasonable collection of Dylan's books as well as various biographies and relevant academic studies, and they are really precious to me.

Thanks in part to his fondness for books and beer, Jack was never flush with funds, and Florrie's difficulties in controlling housekeeping expenditure wouldn't have helped. So in order to supplement the income generated from his teaching post, he gave classes in the Welsh language in the evenings, although he didn't encourage his son to learn the tongue. This was at a time when the Welsh language didn't receive the respect it's achieved in more recent decades. In those harsh times of the early part of the last century when Dylan was growing up, English was generally thought of as an essential tool for economic advancement, and Welsh was regarded as an optional extra. The exact same attitude, and for the same reasons, prevailed in Ireland in relation to the Irish language, although we have not restored Irish to the prominence Welsh now enjoys in many parts of Wales.

Dylan was by no means to be immune from, or unfamiliar with, the attractions of the Welsh tongue. Indeed, many commentators have argued that several of his poems were either based on or inspired by Welsh language rhythms, as, for instance the phrase 'to begin at the beginning' that opens his play *Under Milk Wood.* In fact, Dylan himself admitted to this influence in relation to his poem 'I dreamed my genesis'. Some of his work was to be influenced by what in Welsh language poetry is called 'cynghanedd', a word that means 'harmony' and refers to alliterative patterns that include the repetition of sound and rhyme.

But irrespective of the extent of the influence Welsh was to have on his later work, Jack's son read almost insatiably, becoming familiar with the works of Shakespeare by the time he was about seven, and soon building up an impressive library that included Yeats, Auden, Eliot, DH Lawrence, James Joyce and Virginia Woolf. His literary diet also included Thackeray, William Blake, John Donne and DH Lawrence. His small, dim room, often considerably untidy, contained photographs of his favourite authors, and drawings of the poets Browning and Brooke. He wrote almost as much as he read, lovingly keeping his writings in his famous notebooks, the first of which he started when he was just over fifteen years of age. He claimed that he painstakingly produced only two lines of poetry an hour, and he used Jack's study as well as his own room beside the noisy boiler. He also wrote some of his stories in the house too.

A front window afforded him a view out towards what he described as the '...long and splendid curving shore' of Swansea Bay and the lighthouse at Mumbles. This stretch features in his story 'One Warm Saturday' and its view is reflected in the poem 'Ears in the turrets hear', with its 'ships anchor off the bay'.

Dylan wrote fondly of his childhood in his story 'A Child's Christmas in Wales'. In his early poem 'Upon your held-out hand' he recalled 'When I was seven I counted four and forty trees that stood before my window'. When he wrote that 'the new asylum on the hill leers down the valley like a fool' he was referring to Cefyn Coed asylum, situated about a mile away on a hill overlooking the family home.

Dylan referred to 'Once it was the colour of saying', with its many references to the physical environs of his home, as his 'Cwmdonkin poem'. Indeed, it is estimated that well over half of his published work was at least partly created while he lived here, including such revered works as 'And death shall have no dominion', 'I see the boys of summer' and 'Because the pleasure-bird whistles'. 'On The Marriage of a Virgin' was prompted by his sister Nancy's imminent marriage in 1933. Her husband-to-be was Haydn Taylor. It's hardly a matter of great importance, but I couldn't help spotting the similarity of his first name to my surname

Nancy's Haydn later described the household as a quarrelsome one, with Dylan prone to demanding his own way. Knowing how his mother doted on him, I reckon he probably got it too. His sister had encouraged his writing, although the gap in their ages prevented them from ever being close. If he was annoying her, something that probably occurred fairly often, in order to distract him she would suggest he write a poem about some specific object, maybe an onion, and Dylan would happily set about the task.

In a letter he wrote to her when he was still really a child, the sender's address was given as 'Uplands on Avon', evidence of his familiarity with Shakespeare. The letter opens with the proclamation that 'this is not a news-letter. It is original.' He then goes on to include extracts from poems that show a maturity, and a facility with words, that are way beyond anything one might expect from someone his age at the time.

Dylan himself lived in the house at 'Uplands on Avon'

until 1934, having made his first visit to London in 1933. He would spend much of the rest of his life moving back and forth between England, the USA, and various residences in Wales. The Cwmdonkin house was rented out by the family when they moved to the nearby Gower village of Bishopston in 1937. Regretably, when the Thomases left the house permanently after DJ's retirement after nearly four decades as a teacher, he sold off many of his books. But the house has latterly been restored to much the same condition as when DJ and Florrie originally purchased it as a new dwelling. In what is a rare privilege in the literary world, Thomas fans can now hire the house for self-catering holidays, weekends or overnight stays.

From there it is but a short walk to the attractive seclusion of Cwmdonkin Park to which Dylan was taken not long after his birth, and which was to become very special to him as boy, writer and poet. The park is still very much as it was when he played here among the tall firs with his friends, throwing stones at the swans and teasing 'Old Smalley', the park-keeper John Smallcombe. He once enraged Old Smalley to the point that the keeper hit him on the leg with a spike, drawing blood. But the park was also a place of such unlimited enchantment and wonder as to inspire the descriptive and evocative poems like 'The hunchback in the park'. He wrote about the place in his piece 'Patricia, Edith and Arnold', and its influence is easy to spot in other works too. In 'Especially when the October wind' he notes 'the star-gestured children in the park'. In his radio broadcast *Reminiscences of Childhood* he describes the park as 'full of terrors and treasures', and it also appears in *Return Journey*, his much-loved autobiographical piece for radio. In 'Should lanterns shine' Dylan magically wrote 'The ball I threw while playing in the park has not yet reached the ground'. On many occasions I have sat in the park and wondered about that still hovering ball.

I was delighted when visiting the park in more recent years to note that it now has a shelter named in Dylan's honour and a rough memorial stone engraved with an extract from his later poem 'Fern Hill':

'Oh as I was young and easy in the mercy of his means,
Time held me green and dying
Though I sang in my chains like the sea.'

From when he was about five years of age, Dylan's mother, who was a regular chapel-goer, had taken him regularly to the Congregational Chapel on Walter Road. He was also often encouraged to attend Sunday School at the Paraclete Congregational Church in Newton, near Mumbles. The minister there, the Reverend David Rees, had married Dylan's Aunt Dosie, and had the ability to build up to an impressive level of powerful religious fervour. It is highly probable that Dylan's experiences of the Welsh style of sermonising, in Newton and in other places, encouraged his interest in the poetic potential of the Bible and had a profound bearing on his declamatory vocal style. When

Rees retired, Dylan wrote a tribute to the minister for the *Herald of Wales* newspaper, with a part of it headed 'The End of A Great Ministry.'

Although some commentators see Dylan as a very religious poet, and his writing has many Biblical connections and references, he was never of a conventionally religious bent, as the title of his poem 'The Reverend Crap' should indicate. In his notebook alongside that poem, also sometimes called 'Matthias spat upon the lord', he actually wrote Rees' name, suggesting that his attitude to Uncle David might have been somewhat complex, if not downright contradictory.

After attending a private day school when he was seven, Dylan moved to a school that was run by Mrs Hole at 22 Mirador Crescent, only a few blocks from Cwmdonkin Drive. The school contained a mere two rooms, but was especially popular with parents who harboured ambitions for their offspring. The pupils were required to wear a distinctive uniform, and the school offered regular bible readings, with prayers recited and hymns sung every day. More than likely, Dylan's enrolment was instigated by his mother. Mrs Hole indulged him as much as his mother did, and he was often to be found sitting on the knees of Mrs Hole's daughter who assisted her mother at the school.

This was where he met his long-term friend Mervyn Levy, and also where he heard the 'distant, terrible sad music of the late piano lessons' referred to in *Return Journey*, the upstairs of Mrs Hole's school being used for the teaching of music. He also took part in plays there, and these and other adventures are recounted fondly in *Return Journey* in which the narrator goes back to Swansea and talks to people he believes should remember him, without actually telling them it's his young self he is searching for. A voice in that piece says 'in Mirador School he learned to read and count', and there's also a reference to him filling a girl's galoshes with water. The unfortunate victim thus immortalised was Joyce Daniel from Richmond Road. Another friend at that time was Vera Phillips, who will later re-enter this story as Vera Killick. She once claimed she saw him doing something very rude in the laneway behind the school. Apparently, Dylan was peeing all over a wall and claiming he could write 'God save the king.' It sounds very plausible to me.

Dylan also took elocution lessons with Miss James in Brynymor Crescent.

Just before he was eleven years of age, Dylan started at the nearby Gothic-fronted Swansea Grammar School on Mount Pleasant Hill where his father was Senior English Master. Its motto was, appropriately for both Dylan and his father, 'virtue and good literature', but what remains of that building is now part of Swansea Metropolitan University. Dylan acted in plays while there, wrote poetry for the school magazine, and even became its editor. He also took advantage of the fact that his father was a teacher, and he developed into a quite undisciplined student. He had an indifferent attitude towards most subjects, apart from

English and some sporting activities, and was already beginning to reject the strictures of a formal education. His approach to written examinations was equally distracted. On at least one occasion he enraged his father by answering a totally different question to the one of the paper. He later wrote appreciatively of his father's impressive reading aloud of the works of Shakespeare to classes, but he also used his mother's generally unjustified anxieties about his health to wangle time off school. But there was no faking it when, at the age of twelve, he was knocked down by a bus while cycling on Derwen Fawr to the Swansea regatta in Mumbles. Breaking his wrist, he subsequently underwent two operations in hospital.

His boyish charm, allegedly frail health and his cherubic looks endeared him to many, but Gwevril Dawkins, a friend of Nancy and who used to babysit him, reckoned that had his father not been such a prominent and respected figure at the school, Dylan would almost certainly have been expelled for his unruly behaviour. His school friend Charlie Fisher remembers Dylan towards the end of his school days being so bored that he would burn holes into the floor with a hot poker.

Despite all that, his spell at the Grammar School was beneficial to Dylan on other levels. Through a relationship that first flowered at the school, Daniel Jones became one of Dylan's lifelong friends. Dan lived in a house called Warmley at 38 Eversley Road in Sketty, about a mile from Dylan's home, and was equipped with a piano and other musical instruments. It's widely accepted that Dylan's story 'The Fight' was inspired by their very first, and unpromising, encounter which involved the two of them scrapping in the school playground. Their close relationship serves as further proof of the adage that opposites attract, for while Dylan was prone to be a mischievous clown, Dan was a serious and self-effacing fellow.

Dylan regularly visited the Jones' house to read poems. He also liked to work with Dan on songs and operas, inventing wildly improbably names for the alleged composers of these works. They often became preoccupied with putting together broadcasts for their own imaginary radio station, The Warmley Broadcasting Company. They engaged in many experiments in the various arts for which they both had an aptitude and a deep attraction, although it has been said that Dylan once broke down in tears when he found he could not make sculptures properly. If true, it was one of the few art forms he had tried but could not get to grips with. Although visitors to the Thomas household were not overly encouraged, Daniel visited Cwmdonkin Drive where they produced a journal called *The Era* together. Their juvenile efforts were to prove most fruitful for both of them, as Daniel was to become a highly-rated composer.

When Dylan left the school in 1931, with some help from his father he picked up his first real job as a junior reporter with the *South Wales Daily Post*, the newspaper based in Swansea. Having spent the second half of my career as a writer with *Hot Press*, Ireland's premier rock music magazine, and also having enjoyed a lifelong fascination with the print media, here was another reason for my attraction to Dylan who seemed to aspire to the persona of the stereotypical news hound as depicted in Hollywood movies of the last century.

The *South Wales Daily Post* later changed its name to the *South Wales Evening Post* and was located near Wind Street which Dylan mentioned when he wrote 'I want to have smuts in my eye on Wind Street', and the street is also the setting for his story 'The Followers'. Another story, 'Old Garbo', graphically depicts The Strand area as well as mentioning St Mary's Church in Princess Way. So it's clear that while working on the newspaper Dylan was soaking up the atmosphere of this part of Swansea as raw material for his work. But in the end, his eighteen months with the paper couldn't be described as a runaway success. He didn't even master the basic skill of shorthand essential to all who wanted to ply their trade as newspaper journalists in those days before tape recorders. Of course, working in the bustling and unconventional environment provided by the newspaper industry and its inhabitants must have been a major change for Dylan from the relatively reclusive life of his family

The paper's editor JD Williams regarded him as an unsatisfactory employee, but after his departure from full-time employment with the paper he was still sufficiently attracted to that type of work to carry out some freelance commissions for the publication, penning articles about such topics as the poets of Swansea. The Welsh raconteur Wynford Vaughan-Thomas recalled visiting the Swansea Empire Theatre on Oxford Street with Dylan around this time, and the erstwhile newshound introducing him to the actress Nellie Wallace.

One of Dylan's keenest pleasures was chatting with his artistic friends at the Kardomah Café in Castle Street close to the offices of the *Evening Post*. Legend has it that the Kardomah had been located, by a bizarre coincidence, on the same spot as the church in which Dylan's parents had been married. His regular companions there included Bert Trick, who had a grocery shop on Glanbrydan Avenue, and is referred to in *Return Journey*. Bert's summer house on the Gower peninsula also became a favourite haunt for Dylan, not least because it was close to the sea and afforded him a break from home. The older Bert shared his forthright left-wing views on such matters as religion, politics and social justice with Dylan whose story 'Where Tawe Flows' – Tawe being the river that runs through Swansea and gives the city its Welsh name Abertawe – relates to those get-togethers. A poem in one of Dylan's notebooks called 'Children's Song' has a dedication 'for PT', whom many assume to be Bert's daughter Pamela. Bert or Pamela, depending on whose account you believe, was also the source of the question 'What colour is glory?' which, when he heard it uttered, appealed to Dylan so much that he used it in the line 'Why east wind chills and south wind cools'.

The long-gone Kardomah café, (not to be confused with a newer cafe of the same name situated a few streets away from the older location), was also where he used meet the painters Fred Janes and Mervyn Levy, and his lifelong friend, the poet Vernon Watkins. Among others, they were later immortalised collectively as the Kardomah Gang, and were to be celebrated in a BBC documentary of the same name. In a letter to Charles Fisher Dylan once described the Kardomah as 'home sweet homah'.

It was in Swansea's Bush Hotel that Dylan is believed to have had his last ever drink in Wales. If, as rumoured, it was partaken with Daniel Jones, that would be most appropriate. Daniel had not only been his school chum and artistic collaborator, but a lifelong friend and a creative man whom Dylan respected enough to have often sought his opinion about his own new works.

Not far from Mirador Crescent is The Grove area, which Dylan makes reference to in 'A Fine Beginning', and which was the location of a temporary recording studio where Dylan presented the radio programme *Swansea and the Arts* with some of his Swansea artistic buddies. The building was a church but is now a private residence. The general approach taken by that radio broadcast was later repeated in what was Dylan's first television appearance, the BBC programme *Home Town Swansea*. Many of Dylan's BBC radio broadcasts came from the studios on Alexandra Road, close to what was then his favourite bookshop, Ralph The Books, run by Ralph Wishart. It's not far from the railway station from which Dylan made numerous departures to London and the USA.

Dylan was a customer of the Uplands Cinema where Lloyds Bank later sited a branch, and, although not an overly enthusiastic sportsman in later life, he enjoyed watching cricket at St Helen's rugby and cricket ground, the surrounding area of which is delightfully depicted in the radio play *Holiday Memory*. Perhaps most famously, he enjoyed the camaraderie in pubs and hotels like The Three Lamps, the Singleton Hotel, The Kings Arms and the Uplands Hotel which was just a short walk down from Cwmdonkin Drive. The Uplands is now the Uplands Tavern and on a recent visit I was pleased to discover that it has a designated space known as the Dylan Thomas Snug. DJ used to drink there too, especially when Dylan and Nancy were very young, and I enjoyed a drink in their honour.

One of the city's oldest pubs, the No Sign Bar, was another regular favourite, and it appears in his story 'The Followers' disguised as The Wine Vaults. Dylan was introduced to many of these pubs by his older journalist colleague Freddie Farr, and one of their escapades crop up in 'Old Garbo' in which Farr also appears as a very colourful character, which, by all accounts, he was.

Dylan's lifelong fondness for pubs and drink may, as some maintain, have shortened his life, although his first real girlfriend, the writer Pamela Hansford Johnson remembers him feigning being drunk as if it were an essential part of the image he wished to portray to the world. Dylan's biographer Paul Ferris agreed with this notion, writing in *Dylan Thomas – The Biography* that Dylan 'liked to make comic capital from tales that were only half true or not true at all.' Many people of a conservative mind disapprove of Dylan's bawdy lifestyle and his reputation for drinking, but if he only indulged in those pursuits for a fraction of the alleged time, how could he have produced so much art of such a sublime quality that it has influenced, and continues to influence, an endless number of poets all over the world?

In this regard, Dylan always reminds me of the Dublin writer and playwright Brendan Behan who cultivated an image of the stereotypical drunken Irishman that appealed to many people abroad, even if it provoked a similar opprobrium at home as Dylan's behaviour did. Behan too died young, aged only forty-one, but some of his works, especially the plays *Borstal Boy*, *The Hostage* and *The Quare Fella* are still highly regarded, if rarely staged.

Pamela's observation may have been right about Dylan, but their relationship was not to last. She and her mother actually visited the Cwmdonkin Drive house after she and Dylan started their romance, but the visit was not a success, and the couple soon parted.

Meanwhile, there's no doubting that Dylan enjoyed the physical presence of Swansea, including its numerous pubs, and many streets and buildings are mentioned in his works. In fact, of the ten stories in his collection *Portrait of The Artist As A Young Dog*, six are set in Swansea, two in Gower and another two in Carmarthenshire.

He often took a ramble along the shore of Swansea Bay, and one walk along the beach with his friend Bert Trick inspired the beginnings of the poem 'I see the boys of summer'. Another story, 'Just Like Little Dogs', has him talking about sex to two boys under a railway arch close by the sands. He wrote about dawdling along and exploring around the slaughter-house, gasworks, monuments, the docks and the museum 'that should have been in a museum'.

Later, after he'd enjoyed some success in the wider world, he'd return to Swansea and seek out journalists in order to generate coverage for his achievements in the local newspapers, presumably because he wanted to be thought well of in his native town. This is a further indication of how important Swansea and its people were to him.

Not that all of his hometown experiences were unremittingly positive, even after his worldwide success. He was once invited to speak at the annual dinner organised by the local branch of the British Medical Association but failed to turn up, later explaining his no-show with a, possibly fictitious, tale about the car he was travelling in from London hitting a telegraph pole near Bristol.

Nor did he restrict his formative activities to Swansea town, but he ventured abroad into The Gower peninsula which he described as being 'as beautiful as anywhere', and where he enjoyed camping trips with his school-friends and walking alone along the desolate cliffs 'communing with the cold and quietness'. He cycled about, and took bus rides to

Rhossili along the bay that he described as 'the wildest, bleakest, barrenest' and where he often composed. He enjoyed camping trips there too, and claimed to have had his first full sexual experience, with someone he described a red-mouthed girl, on a weekend visit with a journalist and the journalist's girlfriend.

He enjoyed visiting his friend Vernon Watkins who lived with his parents in Pennard, a village close to the Gower cliffs. Dylan also loved the treacherous Worm Head close by, and on one occasion was trapped there by the incoming tide after he fell asleep. The area infiltrates his stories, such as 'Who Do You Wish Was With Us?' Another story, 'Extraordinary Little Cough', is an almost perfect depiction of a holiday there. It features some of his school chums (including George Hooping, a pun on whose name gives the story its title), plus a group of older girls who had a party and stayed in a nearby tent. It was most likely also the setting for his poem 'We lying by seasand'.

Perhaps most important for his future role as a fine speaker of both prose and poetry was his acting at the Little Theatre in Mumbles, once a separate fishing village about four miles to the south-west of Swansea but integrated into the town as it expanded.

Not that the serious aspects of theatre were Dylan's only preoccupation. Of course he was interested in plays and acting, but he also spared some time for play-acting. After one performance he led the cast up Cefn Bryn ridge to Arthur's Stone, a prehistoric monument in the Gower, apparently inspired by some mischievous notion of invoking the spirits of this mythic place. On another occasion he broke a tooth while playfully pretending to be a dog, an incident that is referenced in *Return Journey*.

His love of drama, as shown by his commitment to the Little Theatre, is reflected in the sonorous voice which, when declaiming poems and stories, became as appealing as their content. Unlike other poets, whose delivery of their own works can seem tepid and listless by comparison, Dylan's delivery has helped enormously to introduce his work to new generations. Some of his admirers are as likely to listen, and re-listen, to his recordings of his work for the pleasure of that voice as much as the poems. I know I do.

His theatrical activities may also have fed the drama and exaggerations that were to become part of his persona, and that feature even in his later letters to friends and colleagues. There are even those who feel he may have harboured serious ambitions to be an actor. To some extent he did actually become an actor, both in public and in private, although not in the conventional sense. One could even regard his whole life as a performance.

Not surprisingly, he was a regular drinker in several pubs around Mumbles, including The Village Inn (called The Marine back in Dylan's day), The Antelope and The Mermaid, and he referred to his 'Mumbles Mermaid (bless her hair and her tail)'. On one of my earliest visits to the town I enjoyed a drink and lunch at the Mermaid, but the area has changed much since then as to be incompatible with my memories. In *Reminiscences of Childhood* Dylan described the pier at Mumbles as having 'skeleton legs', and the lighthouse appears in the story 'Old Garbo', with a reference to a couple making love while looking at it. I remember looking the pier and the lighthouse for the first time and marvelling at what was then to me a totally novel idea, that places you could read about in works of fiction could be real places you could actually visit and look at and maybe even touch.

Bishopston, where his parents lived for a while – at 133 Bishopston Road – after his father's retirement, is in the Gower Peninsula. Dylan and Caitlin often stayed with them at there, and on one visit he wrote his poem 'Ballad of The Long-legged Bait', with its countless sea-related images, and which he described as being about 'a young man fishing for sexual experience'.

He also visited Bert Trick at his holiday home in Caswell Bay, with its sandy beach that could also be reached by foot along a coastal path from Mumbles, and was photographed paddling in the shallow water with Pamela Hansford Johnson with his trousers legs rolled. There's another shot of them playing croquet on the grass near the cliffs at Pennard during a visit to Vernon Watkins. Dylan drank in the Beaufort Arms in the village of Kittle, and the former county of Glamorgan is mentioned in 'Hold hard, these ancient minutes', while there are echoes of the area's landscape in 'A Prospect of the Sea'.

But although most of these places that Dylan found so

fascinating were only minutes away from Swansea, you can't help feeling that it was the heart of Swansea town itself that most attracted and inspired the young Dylan. By his own admission, *Portrait of The Artist As A Young Dog* is all about life in Swansea, an attempt at what he himself described as a 'provincial biography'. Given that he was particularly attracted to the docks area of the town, it's most appropriate that there's now a life-size memorial statue to him in the Maritime Quarter of Swansea. It bears the apt line 'Though I sang in my chains like the sea' from 'Fern Hill', and I found it a little eerie having my photograph taken beside it, wishing it was the real man instead. The statue is located close to the Dylan Thomas Theatre, where the Little Theatre Company is now. It is also close to a statue of the blind Captain Cat, one of the main characters from *Under Milk Wood*, and in nearby Oxford Street there's the Eli Jenkins Pub, named in honour of another character in that play.

Completing what is a veritable Dylan Thomas Quarter is the Dylan Thomas Centre which has hosted such superb and informative attractions as the exhibition entitled *Dylan Thomas: Man And Myth*. I have passed several pleasant afternoons immersing myself in the Centre's Dylan-related artefacts and the audio-visual displays that bring the man to life. It is no doubt helping to open people from all over the globe to explore the literary legacy of one of the towering giants in the literature of the twentieth century. The Centre's cafe and its collection of new and second-hand books are additional attractions to a site that is helping spread the word about Dylan while also serving as another major reason for visiting Swansea. Thus it seems that as time passes, Swansea becomes even more proud of its famous native son. And justifiably so, because the rest of the literary world is doing likewise.

Apart from about eighty poems, all of which were worked on with painstaking commitment to what he described as 'his craft or sullen art', the 'Rimbaud of Cwmdonkin Drive' wrote about forty short stories, a novel, numerous radio talks and several scripts for documentary films. His unique *Under Milk Wood*, an innovative radio play for voices which he set in a vividly imaginary Welsh seaport, was made into a feature film, a cartoon and set to cerdd dant, a unique and traditional Welsh musical form. That play inspired The Beatles producer George Martin to record a star-studded musical version, and was the inspiration for a suite composed by jazz pianist Stan Treacy that has been proclaimed as one of the best British jazz records ever.

As we mentioned earlier, the Welsh poet's name has travelled the world as the adopted name of Bob Dylan, arguably one of the most influential figures of twentiethth century culture and who once appeared on a record under the pseudonym Robert Milkwood Thomas. Now, you might wonder, where did he get that name from?

Dylan's poem 'Do not go gentle into that good night' has become a firm favourite at funerals and on other solemn occasions. A play by Sidney Michaels, and simply called *Dylan*, was produced on Broadway in the mid-sixties. It was partly based on separate books by his American agent John Malcolm Brinnin and Dylan's wife Caitlin Macnamara. His life and times inspired the 1970 novel, also called *Dylan*, by John Summers. In 1982, a plaque was unveiled in his honour in Poets' Corner at Westminster Abbey, although The Prince of Wales is believed to have complained that he hadn't been invited to the event. The annual Dylan Thomas Prize is believed to offer the world's biggest cash prize for young writers, and I was delighted that the 2011 winner was an Irishwoman, Lucy Caldwell from Belfast, who picked up the prize for her novel *The Meeting Point.*

And his influence is not confined to the arts. An Irish horse called Dylan Thomas won the Irish Derby in 2006, and a class 153 locomotive was given the name *Dylan Thomas 1914 – 1953*. But it is still important to be reminded that it all began at the beginning – here in Swansea.

# Dylan's Carmarthenshire Roots

Dylan Thomas' ancestral roots lie in Carmarthenshire, the county to the north-west of his birthplace Swansea and the Gower Peninsula. Carmarthenshire's fine tradition as a Welsh-speaking, chapel-going community made a deep impact on the young Dylan, and, as we have already observed, undoubtedly influenced his poetry as well as his sonorous vocal delivery. And the area was to prove in time to have other, perhaps deeper, resonances for the budding poet and short story writer.

Those ancestral links are concentrated in a triangle formed by the villages of Llangynog, Llangain and Llansteffan which make up what the poet himself described as his 'breeding-box valley'. He spent much of his time in the general area from his boyhood onwards, and during the last years he lived with wife and children in the seaside village of Laugharne which we will deal with separately in a later chapter.

Dylan's father's grandparents lived in Brechfa, and his parents settled in Johnstown where DJ was born. Johnstown is located near to Carmarthen town, and DJ met his future wife Florrie at a fair there, and they married in December, 1903.

Florrie was the youngest child of George and Anna Williams. George had been born on a farm near the River Towy, while Florrie's mother came from a nearby farm called Pen-y-Coed. These farms in Llansteffan later became the setting for Dylan's short story 'A Visit To Grandpa's', and he had a favourite pub called the Edwinsford Arms in Johnstown, although it later closed its doors. After raising their family, George and Anna Williams moved to St Thomas, a working class area in Swansea.

When Dylan's father gave their home in Cwmdonkin Drive the name 'Glanrhyd' he was creating a link back to the house called Glanrhyd y Gwiail, owned by his grandfather, about a dozen miles from Carmarthen town. In giving his son the second name Marlais he may have been thinking of the stream bearing that name in the nearby Cothi Valley.

Many of Dylan's short stories, such as 'The Mouse and the Woman' and the aforementioned 'A Visit To Grandpa's', were inspired by Carmarthenshire, and his enjoyment of the natural surroundings of the open countryside he found there. Although he once wrote to his lifelong friend Vernon Watkins that he was not a 'country man', some of these stirring stories feature the Jarvis Hills and Valley, fictional creations reflecting and inspired by the area's landscape. There are so many of those stories, 'The Tree', 'The Enemies', A Prospect of the Sea', 'The Visitor' and 'The Holy Six' to name just a few, as Dylan set about adapting South Wales as the setting for his creative writings, not dissimilar from the way Thomas Hardy had crafted his fictional Wessex from the south of England. Personally, I find some of his earlier stories a little difficult and mildly unpleasant. There's an unsettling mood about them which he shook off in his later work and into which he infiltrated his sense of fun and of the absurd that brings a levity to them the earlier stories rarely have.

'Fern Hill' is one of Dylan's best loved and most oft-quoted poems, an exuberant expression of a child's delight in the world around him, and in which he graphically recalls being 'young and easy under the apple boughs'. It was inspired by a real place of that name close to Llangain, a modest village situated between Llansteffan and Carmarthen. Any time I've visited the area it's been impossible to do more than look at the house over the barred gate, and it's been hard to know if the house is now occupied, but merely glancing around the surrounding area makes it clear why the young Dylan being entranced by it. In a way, it's not unlike my own boyhood in South County Dublin which was part of the Irish countryside then. Our house was surrounded by fields and looked up at the Three Rock Mountain on which I and my sister Catherine, my brother Jimmy and our various friends treated as if it were our back garden. Not far from our home was a large estate called, would you believe, Fern Hill, owned by the Walker family and in whose grounds a couple of school pals lived. Although in adulthood I resided for a while in suburbia, I now live among the fertile fields of County Wexford in a refreshingly rustic environment not unlike that surrounding Dylan's Fern Hill.

The Fern Hill house looks down on a tree-clad valley. It was built in 1723, and the farm was owned by Dylan's Aunt Annie with whom he shared a mutual fondness. The young Dylan enjoyed many school holidays here with Annie and his Uncle Jim, exploring the surroundings, and enjoying the fishing and other stimulating activities. He describes it as 'a lively farm' and 'a lonely farm'. The place was rundown and somewhat untidy, with an earthy life to it. The house is supposed to have once been in the possession of the former Carmarthen hangman Robert Evans, a fact that no doubt appealed to Dylan's mischievous and often morbid imagination, especially when you add the well-circulated story that Evans had inserted bars in the lower windows of the house to keep his daughter in and prevent her from meeting her boy-friend. When she escaped, Evans is reputed to have hanged himself in the kitchen.

Fern Hill also features under the name Gorse Hill as the setting for the story 'The Peaches' which was one of Dylan's own favourites. It's a creative blending of several boyhood holidays, and he described it as 'a long story about my true childhood'. That tale connected back to a real-life visit to the farm by a family friend Jack Williams and his mother. The mother, who lived near Cwmdonkin Drive, and whom Dylan described as being fitted out like a ship, was not impressed by her portrayal when she read Dylan's writing. The tale also includes Dylan's Uncle Jim, Aunt Annie and their son Gwilym who appears as the hellfire-preaching Idris practicing his sermonising from a farm cart.

Annie was so very dear to him that his poem 'After the funeral' (In Memory of Ann Jones) was directly inspired by her death in 1933, and he refers to himself in it as 'Ann's bard'. Introducing his reading of it for BBC radio, Dylan admitted that it was the only poem he'd written that was directly concerned with the life and death of one particular person he knew. In that evocative poem, Dylan described the front room of Annie's house having its 'stuffed fox and stale fern', and refers to her as 'humped Ann'. She's buried close by in Llanybri, and Dylan described her as 'sculptured Ann' when writing in his notebook shortly after her funeral. Coincidentally, there has been some speculation that the spire referred to in the poem 'The spire cranes' could have been the ruined tower of the church in Llanybri, close to which Ann's grace is located. From there you can see the Boathouse in Laugharne, from where Dylan in turn also had sight of the same spires.

Dylan's mother's folks came from Llangain, and her brother Tom owned a stone cottage called Blaencwm. Dylan stayed in Blaencwm regularly from an early age, visiting various family members, including his Aunt Ann after she moved here from Fern Hill, as well as his Uncle David Rees and Aunt Theodosia. He wrote poetry at Blaencwm from as early as his teenage years, and it is generally accepted that it was here that he completed 'Fern Hill', plus other poems, including a rewriting of 'Unluckily for a death'. He wrote his nostalgic talk *Memories of Christmas* here too, and also wrote to Pamela Hansford Johnson, 'I can smell the river and hear the beastly little brook that goes gurgle-gurgle past this room...'

The poems he composed while in the area included some of the works that were to be published in his collection *18 Poems* in 1934. One of those works was 'Before I knocked', and some believe that the reference to 'the water that shaped the Jordan near my home' relates to the belief held by a local farmer that the stream that ran by his cottage consisted of water from the Jordan in the Holy Land. 'In the beginning' and 'My hero bares his nerves' were also written in Llangain.

After Dylan's Aunt Theodosia and Uncle David had passed away, his parents moved to live in Blaencwm, and in the mid forties Dylan and Caitlin came to stay with them there in the already cramped cottage. Dylan also stopped over with his father at the cottage while Florence was in hospital in Carmarthen in 1948 after having broken her leg. Of particular delight for DJ were the times that he and Dylan spent together trying to solve *The Times'* crossword, a major pastime of DJ's, as they were also to do together later in Laugharne. Dylan's sister Nancy joined them in Blaencwm for a time. She had by now divorced Haydn Taylor and married Gordon Summersby, but she irritated Dylan who described her as 'hockey-voiced'. From here too he despatched a pleading, apologetic letter to Caitlin with whom his relationship was going through one of its many crises.

Years later, Florence and a Mrs Hettie Owen were clearing out a cupboard in the cottage at Blaencwm when they stumbled upon a collection of Dylan's documents that included manuscripts of some early poems, including 'The Mishap' and The Maniac'. Florence gave them to Hettie, and they were subsequently passed to a research centre in Texas.

Later, while living in Laugharne, Dylan often visited Carmarthen town on shopping expeditions or to go to the cinema with Caitlin. Carmarthen is like many Irish market towns, such as Wexford, Ballina or Westport, with its relaxed sense of business and its colour, so it's a town I feel very much at ease in. Just before his ill-fated trip to the USA, he fainted while they were watching a film there, at least according to the story put about by his mother. But a Doctor Hughes from St Clears, who also happened to be attending the film at the same time, disputed this account of what happened. He claimed that he had agreed to examine Dylan, who was supposedly complaining of headaches, after they got back to his house, but when the film ended and the lights went on they realised that Dylan had disappeared. It's quite possible that he had absconded to the Boar's Head pub which he was known to like very much, although the family were once asked to leave the premises because their son Llewelyn was making a nuisance of himself with the other customers. In a letter written from Llangain, Dylan humorously referred to the inhabitants of the village going into the pubs sideways, presumably because of their portliness, and from here he posted Vernon Watkins a copy of 'Poem in October' for his perusal and comments. On returning after their later sojourn in New Quay, Dylan fondly wrote in a letter about the cottage's 'parlour with a preserved sheepdog, where mothballs fly at night .... and the Bible opens at Revelations...'

The area was of such importance to Dylan that when the Texas-born photographer Rollie McKenna came over from the USA to Laugharne to take photographs of Dylan for *Mademoiselle* magazine, the photographer and the poet travelled with Florence to various places in Carmarthenshire. Their trip included a grand tour of the Fern Hill buildings, and visits to the graveyard at Llanybri and the Blaencwm cottages, with Dylan agreeing to pose wherever McKenna requested him to. These illuminating photographs, as well as others taken showing family members, friends and places associated with the poet, were later published in McKenna's admirable book *Portrait of Dylan*. The series of photos in that book alone show how close the area was to Dylan's heart and why it played such an influential role in his life and art. It's well worth exploring to gather some sense of where Dylan, and much of his work, dreamed their genesis.

# New Quay
# An Interlude in West Wales

The 2008 film *The Edge Of Love*, starring Matthew Rhys as Dylan Thomas and Sienna Miller as his wife Caitlin, focused on a serious incident that occurred when Dylan was staying in the west Wales seaside town of New Quay. This short phase in the poet's life was also dramatised in the play *Badgers In My Vest* by John Fletcher and broadcast on BBC radio.

Before they moved to New Quay, Dylan and Caitlin had resided in other places not too far away; Between 1941 and 1943, while Dylan travelled up to London for work, they lived in Plas Gelli at Talsarn near Lampeter, little more than ten miles away. Plas Gelli was owned by Vera Killick who, as Vera Phillips, had lived near the Thomas house in Swansea's Uplands and, as we shall see, whose husband was to play a central role the story dramatised in *The Edge Of Love*. Dylan had known her before she was married and she'd been one of the few women to have occasionally infiltrated the virtually all-male Kardomah Gang in Swansea.

Dylan particularly liked the Aeron valley around the comparatively remote village Talsarn, describing it as 'the most precious place in the world'. His poem 'A Winter's Tale' can be read as an invocation of the valley, and the River Aeron gave their daughter Aeronwy her first name. He worked on his documentary film scripts while at Plas Gelli, and his poem 'Love In the Asylum' may have been partly inspired by a spirit that was reputed to haunt the house, although others read it as a description of Caitlin's role as his muse. During his spell here, Dylan was particularly fond of writing while sitting under a redwood tree that grew close by. The Red Lion pub (later called Llew Coch) was another favourite spot of his.

While maintaining his base there, the poet occasionally took a break away from Plas Gelli and stayed at the Castle Hotel in Lampeter. He found its landlord Edward Evans very personable and much to his liking, and he also approved of the unpretentious surroundings of the bar there. He liked strolling in the college grounds in Lampeter too, and is reputed to have sung Welsh hymns with the local rugby team.

The Thomases also stayed in the village of Talgarreg, also inland from New Quay, for a short spell in 1942. Talgarreg was the home of Dewi Emrys, one of Wales' most respected bards. While in the area he would also visit the Three Horseshoes pub in Llangeitho.

So in 1944, shortly after Aeronwy was born, they came to New Quay, to an area Dylan had first visited just before the outbreak of the Second World War in the company of the painter Augustus John. Its location on the coast offered a broad prospect out over Cardigan Bay that must have appealed to Dylan as such places often did. He and Caitlin were to stay here for a little more than a year that included one of the coldest winters on record, taking up residence in a small timber and asbestos bungalow called Majoda. As short of money as ever, they rented it for £1 a week. Now long gone, the bungalow had to be recreated in a nearby field for the filming of scenes for *The Edge Of Love*.

When it was still standing, Majoda was located in Plas Llanina, and only a brisk walk from the quaint town of New Quay itself. By no means averse to local attractions such as The Black Lion pub, Dylan had other reasons for relocating his family to this remote area, as he was also keen to avoid a war that he loathed. The Majoda bungalow had marvellous views of the sea and gave them access to a beach and a town with enough pubs, people, activity and talk. It made an ideal retreat for him, and a productive one too in terms of his creative output, as he composed or finished several poems here that found their way into his collection *Deaths and Entrances*. There are few who can doubt that he derived much inspiration from a place he once described as 'a cliff-perched town at the far end of Wales'.

New Quay was one of the first placed associated with Dylan that I visited sometime back in the seventies. I remember it well because I was a bit of a late starter as an imbiber of alcohol, certainly by Dylan's standards and in comparison to my friends and acquaintances in Ireland, but it was in the Black Lion that I first got drunk. Not that I wish to boast about this, but I'd gone there with a couple of holidaying Irish companions whom I'd convinced their lives wouldn't be worth living if they passed up the opportunity to enjoy a pint or two in this famous pub. I remember the bar full of people and noisy chat and a large dog spread out before a blazing fire. At the time I had a dark beard and a local man came in, pointed over at me, and proclaimed 'It's Jesus Christ!', prompting loud cheering and good-natured guffaws from the assembly. This made me feel at ease and it seemed like something a character in Dylan's company or in *Under Milk Wood* might say. Happy to spend an hour or two among such an animated and cheery crowd, I over-indulged in draught pints of Newcastle Brown Ale. At one point I stood up suddenly and cracked my head on a bell on the wall. It peeled loudly, and another member of the crowd shouted, 'he's won the No-bel prize!'

Later, in a vain attempt to prove my sobriety, I walked along the white line down the middle of the road that overlooked the harbour and on which our guest house was located. Safely inside, I lay back on my bed and could see various coloured lights flashing in the sky through the bay window. I remember thinking that if this is what getting drunk is all about, no wonder it's so popular!

Next morning the landlady of the house tried to relieve my throbbing head with a concoction of hot water, lemon and honey, and while I was recuperating I heard on the radio that the local coastguard had been called out during the night to look for a vessel in trouble and that had sent flares up into the sky. So much for my assumption that large quantities of ale came with a free kaleidoscopic lightshow! Still, I hope Dylan would have approved.

Not that he spent all his time at the Black Lion. To avoid the distraction of holidaying children, Dylan often removed himself to the Apple House near Majoda to work on such compositions as 'The conversation of prayers', 'A Refusal To Mourn the Death, By Fire, of a Child in London' and 'A Winter's Tale'. This refuge was part of the estate of Plas Llanina, owned by Lord Howard de Walden to whom Dylan was introduced by Augustus John back in the thirties. De Walden, a keen supporter of the arts, had previously given money to Dylan, and generously permitted the poet to use his Apple House, a small stone building at the edge of his walled garden, as a writing room, a precursor to Dylan's writing shed in Laugharne. Dylan gladly accepted. The shed, as the one behind the Laugharne Boathouse would later, gave him a respite from the irritating hubbub of family life and a quiet place where he could concentrate on his writing. Its proximity to the sea is another parallel with Laugharne and the fictitious Llaregub of *Under Milk Wood*, and while the Majoda house was long ago demolished to make way for a new bungalow, the Apple House is still standing.

While visiting New Quay with my friend Wyn Jones from Cardigan we explored the area and the site where

Majoda used to be. Later, we were generously shown around the grounds of Llas Llanina by the present occupant, and it was easy to imagine why the Apple House served as such an attractive refuge for Dylan. It was a remarkably quiet spot, not far from the sea but cut off from even the closest activity.

Vera Killick and her overwrought husband William lived close by Majoda in a villa known as Ffynnonfeddyg, having moved there from Plas Gelli. The unpleasant incident, on which the film *The Edge of Love* is based, involved Dylan, Caitlin and the Killicks, with William taking a starring role. He had just returned from active war service with the British Army in Greece, and he took exception to his wife consorting with the Thomases. He may even have suspected that Vera was having a relationship with Dylan, as they'd known each other from their childhood days in Swansea, but most likely he was upset because his wife had been spending some of his wages on Dylan and Caitlin.

One day while Dylan was entertaining some visiting film industry friends in The Commercial pub in New Quay, a row developed during which soldier Killick verbally abused Dylan and his companions over their non-combative attitude to war. This was in some ways unfair, as Dylan had more or less been deemed unfit for war service, and had written film scripts that were part of the Ministry of Information's war effort, although Killick probably had little way of knowing about any of this. Nor would Killick have known how the First World War had impacted on Dylan's poetry, such as 'I dreamed my genesis', or that in 1936 he'd published 'The hand that signed the paper', now regarded as a classic anti-war poem.

Later that same evening, Dylan and Killick's paths crossed again at the Black Lion. This time a more aggressive confrontation ensued, with further hostile exchanges and some reports of Killick striking Dylan's female friend Fanya Fisher. Dylan was rescued from further unpleasantness through the intervention of a local friend, Alistair Graham, who took him away from the scene. The two arrived back at Majoda thinking they were safe and that the day's tricky business had ended. But not so. Killick arrived soon after, and, in a fury, set about threatening the bungalow with a machine-gun and a grenade. Fortunately, his one-man assault raid was rather inept and proved, thankfully, to be unsuccessful. Dylan allegedly disarmed him in heroic style, and little damage was done, apart from some bullet holes in the walls of the bungalow. Killick was subsequently charged with attempted murder, and Dylan gave evidence at the trial at Lampeter Assizes. The soldier was acquitted, and there was some suggestion that he was unstable at the time, but the incident definitely rattled Dylan. Naturally, it didn't take long for the episode to become a major gossiping point in the area, with increasingly less regard for the facts of the matter as time went by. Still, it has always puzzled me as to why this particular episode in Dylan's life was singled out for special treatment in a film when there are so many better options to choose out of his rambunctious life.

But the difficulties of his sojourn at Majoda were not restricted to noisy kids and being shot at. Dylan is also believed to have raised the ire of his benefactor's housekeeper Kathleen Davies by making unwanted passes at her. Legend has it that in retaliation she burned, or otherwise destroyed, some of his papers. She is buried in the grave close by the church.

Ffynnonfeddyg, the house then occupied by the Killicks, is a short walk from the quaint St Ina's Church which Dylan and Caitlin passed on their occasional rambles. While at Majoda, Dylan also took the time to visit the pubs in outlying places such as Llangeitho, Llanon and Llangrannog, as well as several of those he liked in New Quay.

Caitlin said that 'This side of the truth' was composed here for their son Llewelyn, and indeed it bears the dedication 'for Llewelyn' under the title. Dylan did some of his best writing during his stay in Majoda, including the descriptive *Quite Early One Morning*, a fore-runner to *Under Milk Wood*, with its reference to the Black Lion as a 'pink washed pub'. Caitlin actually described the pub as being more homely than their own home. In 1944 Dylan sent Tommy Earp a letter in the form of a poem in which he writes fondly of New Quay, The Black Lion, Buckley's mild beer, Worthington's beer and 'Mr Jones the Cake'. In another letter to Earp, Dylan told him about Majoda, on 'the Welsh-speaking sea', and explained his intention to stay there until the war was over.

He and Caitlin could stroll the mile from Majoda to the steep streets of New Quay though the since-eroded Brongwyn Lane, back then a popular spot for courting couples and thought by many to be the origin of Goosegog Lane in *Under Milk Wood*. In fact David N Thomas, in his book *The Dylan Thomas Trail*, suggests as much. Along the lane was Maesgwyn Farm, and the poet mentions Maesgwyn in the early part of *Under Milk Wood* when the Fifth Drowned Character wonders 'Who milks the cows in Maesgwyn?' Critic John Ackerman has suggested that the voices of the drowned sailors in the opening section of the play came from the real story of a drowned graveyard that once existed at Llanina. Other aspects of Llanina may be found in some verses of his poem 'Ballad of the Long-legged Bait'.

Close to the harbour in New Quay is London House, once a shop and the home of Norman Evans, a friend of Dylan's. Apparently, Norman was not too enthusiastic in his attitude to work, and is said to be the basis for Nogood Boyo in *Under Milk Wood*. Near the entrance to the harbour is the toilet, its environs a regular haunt where sailors would gather for a chat. It's hard to imagine Dylan not joining them. In Church Street is the Dolau, a pub claimed to a favourite of Caitlin's, and located close to the Blue Bell where Dylan drank with the Welsh actor Richard Burton. Further up Glanmor Terrace is the site of the post office from which Dylan sent his work to London. The postman back then was Jack Lloyd, the alleged inspiration for Willy Nilly in *Under Milk Wood*. Like Willy, Jack was reputed to indulge in the habit of opening people's letters before delivering them to their intended recipients.

Further along is the aforementioned Black Lion which was owned at the time by Dylan's friend Jack Pat. Apart from the site of Majoda, the Black Lion has probably been the most essential site for Dylan pilgrims drawn to visit New Quay over the years. There's a section of his radio broadcast entitled *The Crumbs of One Man's Year* which enables the listener to imagine Dylan walking from Majoda to the town and the Black Lion 'where the cat purred like a fire'. In recent decades visitors could admire the pub's impressive display of photos and souvenirs of the poet.

On the other side of the road is Gomer House, the home of Captain Tom Polly, suggested by several observers as the original of Captain Cat. Tom lived in Schooner Town, while the fictional captain resided in Schooner House. Now that's hardly a coincidence, is it? By the top of the hill is the Seahorse Inn, once known as the Sailor's Home Arms, a fact that prompted its declaration to be the original of *Under Milk Wood's* Sailor's Arms. Dylan was once allegedly spotted there listening to the live jazz music provided by the pianist Dill Jones. The minister of the nearby Towyn Chapel, the Rev Orchwy Bowen, was a poet and preacher, and himself the father of two noted poets, so he may have inspired the Rev Eli Jenkins character.

A tree-clad lane leads to Wendowel, the home of

Dylan's Aunty Elizabeth Williams and his cousin Theodosia Legg whom he had called on back in the thirties. In George Street, beside Bethel Chapel, was a house called Arnant, a cobblers in which Dylan enjoyed many a lively chat with the locals, the company often including his temporary landlord and benefactor Lord Howard de Walden. Near to it was Manchester House, then a drapers like the one in *Under Milk Wood*, although a house of the same name in Laugharne could make a similar claim to fame. The old police station, described by Dylan in *Quite Early One Morning* as 'black as a helmet, dry as a summons', is claimed as the prototype for the play's Handcuff House. Its then policeman-in-residence, PC Islwyn Williams, has been offered as the inspiration for the play's PC Attila Rees. Williams, incidentally, was a witness in the Killick/Majoda court hearing in Lampeter.

New Quay is maybe a dozen miles from Llandysul, where lived Dylan's great-uncle Gwilym Marles, a firebrand Unitarian preacher and poet with whom Dylan shared a name, and, perhaps, inherited more than a little of his bombastic delivery. Some commentators believe that the character Rev Eli Jenkins in *Under Milk Wood* was fondly based on him rather than on Rev Orchwy Bowen.

The fictional Cherry Owen from the play can more convincingly be traced to a Dan 'Cherry' Jones, a builder who was based in the town and was the son-in-law of a drinking companion of Dylan's called Walter Cherry. In one of his early versions of the play, Dylan referred to the character as Cherry Jones, scoring a point for New Quay against Laugharne in the great debate as to which location was the topographical basis for his play and where its most colourful characters must have originated.

Indeed, the accumulation of the aforementioned links, plus others too numerous to cover in a publication of this size, has led to enthusiastic local claims that New Quay was beyond doubt the real inspiration for the setting and population of *Under Milk Wood*. But it's more likely that several of the places that Dylan visited, or lived in, fed his fevered imagination and helped him make one composite creation. It's highly unlikely that we will ever know for certain, but in the meantime there's much fun to be had weighing up the claims made for various towns having been the basis for Llaregub, with New Quay undoubtedly one of the leading contenders. It's a lively, colourful town and one that I always enjoy revisiting, but on my last visit I was disappointed to find the Black Lion closed and up for sale, so I had to forgo another fireworks display! Maybe on my next visit?

*5 Cwmdonkin Drive in the Uplands, Swansea.*

*The room at 5 Cwmdonkin Drive in which Dylan was born.*
*The current curators of the house, Geoff and Anne Haden, have restored the*
*house to what it looked like when Dylan lived here.*

*Dylan's own room.*

*The living room at 5 Cwmdonkin Drive.*

*Typewriter and bookshelf at 5 Cwmdonkin Drive.*

*A gramophone player in 5 Cwmdonkin Drive.*

*The memorial stone to Dylan in Cwmdonkin Park engraved with lines from his poem 'Fern Hill'.*

*Cwmdonkin Park, a short walk from the Thomas household and where the boy Dylan spent so much of his formative years. The view includes the Dylan Thomas Memorial Shelter.*

*The pier at Mumbles near Swansea.*

*One of the many views of Newquay that Dylan would have enjoyed while he lived at Majoda.*

*The Black Lion in Newquay, one of Dylan's favourite pubs.*

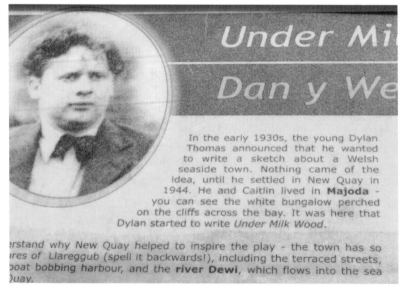

Under Mi

Dan y We

In the early 1930s, the young Dylan Thomas announced that he wanted to write a sketch about a Welsh seaside town. Nothing came of the idea, until he settled in New Quay in 1944. He and Caitlin lived in **Majoda** - you can see the white bungalow perched on the cliffs across the bay. It was here that Dylan started to write *Under Milk Wood*.

erstand why New Quay helped to inspire the play - the town has so ures of Llareggub (spell it backwards!), including the terraced streets, boat bobbing harbour, and the **river Dewi**, which flows into the sea Quay.

*A sign on the Dylan Thomas Trail in Newquay.*

*Towyn Chapel. When Dylan lived near Newquay, the Minister was both a preacher and a poet, and a serious candidate for the original of the Reverend Eli Jenkins in Under Milk Wood.*

*The Dolau Inn in Newquay that Caitlin used to frequent.*

*Ffynnonfeddyg, the house where Dylan's friend Vera Killick
and her ill-tempered husband William lived.*

*The door of Plas Llanina, near Newquay, which leads to the
Apple House where Dylan wrote some of his best work.*

*The sea view from near Majoda. Dylan loved living by the sea, and his name can be translated from the Welsh as "sea son of the wave".*

*The Sea Horse in Newquay, formerly known as the Sailor's Home Arms and one of several sites said to have been the inspiration for the Sailor's Arms in Under Milk Wood.*

*Fern Hill near Carmarthen Town, as it is today. Dylan spent many happy summer holidays here as boy, and it inspired his famous poem of the same name.*

*The Boat House in Laugharne.*

*The centre of Laugharne today, with the Clock Tower and the Castle in the background.*

*Dylan Walk, connecting the Boat House and Brown's Hotel.*

*Brown's Hotel.*

*Dylan's writing shed behind and above the Boat House,
with a view across the estuary to Sir John's Hill.*

*The interior of Dylan's writing shed, with his table
beside the window facing across the estuary.*

*Pelican in Laugharne, which Dylan rented for his parents and where his coffin rested before his funeral.*

*Dylan's final resting place in the graveyard
of St Martin's Church, Laugharne.*

*Statue of Dylan close by the Dylan Thomas Centre in Swansea.*

*Dylan's final resting place in the graveyard
of St Martin's Church, Laugharne.*

# In Country Heaven

The nature of Dylan's work meant that he spent a lot of his time in London where most of the media and book publishing houses were based. He also undertook four reading trips to the USA, during which many observers were enthralled or otherwise by what might have been their first experience of a real-life, larger-than-life Celtic poet and personality.

He also visited Italy, Persia (now called Iran) and the country then known as Czechoslovakia. He enjoyed holiday trips to Ireland, where his wife Caitlin, although born in London, grew up, and spent time in Penzance in Cornwall where they married. His need to find a place to work, live and raise a family, while remaining close to the nub of the publishing world, took him to various parts of England.

Yet amid all the busyness of his comparatively short life and his prolific working career, Dylan journeyed back whenever he could to the Welsh places he loved. While some have castigated Dylan for being somewhat anti-Welsh, there's ample evidence that he loved his Wales and his Welshness. Indeed it's impossible to read much of his work without coming upon aspects of Wales time and time again.

Wales is mentioned by name twice in his poem 'Prologue', and in his poem 'After the funeral' he refers to 'the parched world of Wales'. 'The lubber crust of Wales' occurs in 'Once below a time'. Y Cyfarwydd, the Welsh tradition of the storyteller, must also have been at work in Dylan's decision to take for himself the role of First Voice in the first live performances of *Under Milk Wood* in New York.

When he and Caitlin started their family, their first two children were given Welsh first names, Llewelyn and Aeronwy. The latter was named after the River Aeron, beside which she is reputed to have been conceived. The third and last child Colm, a very common name in Ireland, had Garan as his second name, that being the Welsh word for 'heron', a bird with which the poet often seemed to identify.

The distinguished poet and Welsh-speaking nationalist Saunders Lewis said that Dylan 'brought honour to Wales, and in his later years became more and more Welsh in his sympathies.' The English critic Geoffrey Moore said that Dylan 'went back to South Wales because his heart was there and because his themes of life and death and love were mostly conceived in terms of the people, the places and the institutions of south Wales'.

I would not have developed such an interest in Wales if the impressions I picked up through Dylan work and comments were as negative as some people assume. I see it in Ireland quite a lot, when tribal insecurities lead people to bristle and take serious personal offense whenever their native village, town or country, or indeed the country as a whole, is criticised. Yes, it's pleasant to hear the places we hold dear spoken well of, but they are unlikely to be perfect.

Of course, Dylan could be as wittily dismissive of his Welsh compatriots as he was of himself, but rarely with malice, in my view. This is common in Ireland too, where people who would never contemplate living anywhere else are likely to denigrate the country, its people and its culture. To me it's an affectation, and sometimes an unpleasant one at that, but it's more of a casual part of the national conversation rather than expressing views that are meant to be taken seriously. It may even be therapeutic for some, and it can be highly entertaining when wit is mixed with a little wisdom.

That said, many of Dylan's comments and observations may have been fuelled by alcohol, and while that is not an entirely acceptable excuse, they are not recommended for those of a sensitive nature. For Dylan, sacred cows existed to be milked, and he often did just that, often with genuine gusto and unbridled glee. There were many who were disturbed to find that his fictitious village Llaregub when spelled backwards becomes a vulgar phrase once thought of as totally unsuitable for genteel company. But now we can see it as an example of his wit, his playfulness with words and his pleasure in mischief-making. His sense of humour, his love of the absurd and his penchant for self-mockery made him an engaging, entertaining and lively companion.

So, apart from the forays that necessarily took him away, the poet spent nearly all of his life in his native country, Indeed, there is little evidence of Dylan wanting to live anywhere other than Wales, and he visited many places besides those I've already alluded to.

Welsh places names abound in his writing, including the poem 'Request to an obliging Poet' which mentions maids from Kidwelly, lasses from Bangor, naiads from Narberth, nymphs from Pwlldu, gnomes from Llanllwch and elves from Llansamlet.

For a long time he actually toyed with the notion of writing a travel book in which he would visit painters and artists who lived in various parts of the country, and journeyed to Machynlleth and Aberystwyth as part of his research. There were holidays in Wales too, of course, and trips away with his father. When Dylan was about three, the family went to a boarding-house in Llandrindod Wells for a holiday. In 1929 he travelled with his father to Abergavenny to visit the recently-married Doris Williams. Her husband Randolph provided Dylan with an opportunity to exhibit his impish wit when Randolph nearly crashed the car on the way back from a trip to the Brecon Beacons, prompting Dylan to quip, 'Lovely, Uncle. Can we go back and do it again?'

In 1930 Dylan took a break with his school friend Cyril

James to St Dogmael's, near Cardigan, where Cyril's relatives had a farm called Yr Hendre overlooking Cardigan Bay. The visit inspired some of Dylan's more juvenile poetry, including some lines about a girl he met there called Chloe and which he wrote into an autograph album for Bonnie James who lived at the farm. That album later travelled up along the coast when it came into the possession of the National Library of Wales in Aberystwyth. I've been to that magnificent library and was very impressed with its range of books and documents, but, not having known about the autograph album, I didn't seek it out, but I will next time. Dylan was to revisit Cardigan a number of times in later life, including a trip to an agricultural fair in 1944 at which he met Dot, the sister of Vernon Watkins. On one of those visits he went to Cross Inn and wrote a naughty poem (called 'Sooner than you can water milk') about the pub there.

Although Dylan never learned to drive, and cycling and walking were not as high on his list of activities in his adult life as they had been in his youth, the kindness of car-owning friends, such as the Pembrokeshire-born painter Augustus John, enabled him to see more of Wales than he might otherwise have done.

Dylan attended the eisteddfod in Fishguard in 1936, and that town, which links Wales by daily ferry to Caitlin's Ireland, was also the location for the filming of his play for voices *Under Milk Wood*, starring Richard Burton, Elizabeth Taylor and Peter O'Toole (Welsh, English and Irish respectively). Fishguard was an apt choice for the filming, as the setting for the dawn-sequence in the play is believed to have been inspired by the Druid stones that overlook the old harbour of that pleasant town which I've visited many times myself. Indeed, on one occasion I took the ferry over from Rosslare in Ireland, and enjoyed a fine lunch in Myles Pepper's restaurant at the West Wales Art Centre. I then travelled back home the same day, all for no other reason that the satisfaction of saying that I'd gone over to Fishguard for lunch!

When Dylan was returning from one trip to Fishguard with Augustus John and the then-single Caitlin Macnamara, the trio stopped for a drink at the Boar's Head in Carmarthen. A jealous row ensued between Dylan and John over Caitlin, resulting in Dylan being knocked to the ground.

During the war, Dylan was called to Llandeilo, near Carmarthen, so that he could undergo an army medical check-up. He had pleaded against being called up for active service on account of his ill-health, although he was also known to loathe the war, and expressed such loathing in some poems. He is reported to have attended the check-up in a state of inebriation, and was given the C3 status which meant that, although he was technically fit for service, he was in such poor condition that the British Army would have to be desperate for recruits before he would ever be enlisted.

Aberystwyth is mentioned in a number of Dylan's works, and a hymn of that name is sung by Cherry Owen in *Under Milk Wood*. Dylan visited the town in 1934 with his fellow-writer Glyn Jones to have tea with one of Dylan's favourite writers, the irreverent satirist Caradoc Evans. In his story 'Where Tawe Flows', Dylan has one of his characters refer to 'the great Caradoc Evans'. Dylan was a keen admirer of Evans whose influence can be seen in the more surreal aspects of Dylan's stories. During the visit, either Evans or Jones told Dylan the tale of a Dr Price who claimed to be a druid and was also a champion of cremation. He had a son born out of wedlock and called him Jesus Christ. When the child died at the age of five, Price burned the body on a hilltop in the Caerlan fields in Llantrisant. The meeting inspired Dylan's short story 'The Burning Baby'.

That wasn't the only fire-related incident of that momentous trip. When they stayed overnight in a local hotel, Dylan inadvertently burned holes in his bed sheets through careless smoking. In 1937 Dylan visited Evans again. In 1953 came here especially to give a poetry recital, and stayed with Glyn Jones at his place on Bryn-y-Mor Road.

Dylan came to Gilfachreda, a short distance from New Quay, to visit Alistair Graham. He was an oboe player and close friend of the writer Evelyn Waugh and of the arts patron Lord Tredegar, and lived in Plas y Wern. During a party at Graham's house Dylan and Augustus John indulged in a spot of mutual name-calling that amused some guests and disgusted others.

Dylan's interest and expertise in the art of film has been somewhat lost over the decades, perhaps overshadowed by the quality and volume of his poetry and short story output.

He wrote the dialogue for the film *Three Weird Sisters*, a tale about three women from the Welsh valleys. In 1942, a short break away in Cardiganshire gave Dylan some material for the film documentary *Wales – Green Mountain, Black Mountain* which he scripted and produced, and the mines of South Wales featured in his documentary *Our Country*. In 1950 he went to Pendine Sands to visit the set of the film *Pandora And the Flying Dutchman*. The Rebecca riots, organised in protest against toll road fees, took place in Pembrokeshire, Cardiganshire and Carmarthenshire in the middle of the nineteenth century and formed the basis for the film *Rebecca's Daughters*, for which Dylan also penned the script.

While living for a time in this area he drank in the Central Hotel in Llanon with his friend, the vet Thomas Herbert who often invited Dylan to join him in his car as he made his round of calls as part of his veterinary duties. He also took Dylan out in his motor to show him the attractions of the local Cardiganshire countryside, and Dylan's poem 'In Country Sleep' is redolent of the landscape around here.

Herbert was very fond of literature in both Welsh and English, and his bilingualism was useful to Dylan who would often ask him to give him the English translations of the names of Welsh places. Close to Llanon lay Wernllaeth Farm, whose name is of particular interest to Dylan's fans because 'wernllaeth' can be translated from the Welsh as 'milk alder grove', yet another possible source for the naming of *Under Milk Wood*. The pair visited the Ship

Inn in Llangrannog too.

His story 'The Outing' is about an aborted day trip by charabanc to Porthcawl, visiting various pubs along the way. Dylan visited Cardiff too, although not always with memorable success. He was once invited by his lecturer friend Mervyn Levy to dinner in the Welsh capital in the house owned by a psychiatrist friend of Levy's. By all reports, it was no social triumph. An even more unfortunate visit to Cardiff resulted in Dylan, not for the only time, losing his precious manuscript of *Under Milk Wood* at the Park Hotel. So, not all of Dylan's travels in Wales were positive experiences. When his father was cremated in Glyntaff Crematorium in Pontypridd, the occasion caused great distress to Dylan. A breeze blew the smoke in a swirl around the grieving son, making him imagine he was breathing in his father's remains. It made him feel extremely ill.

During one of the trips his American tour manager made to Wales, they travelled together as far as St David's on the Pembrokeshire coast not far from Fishguard, visiting the impressive cathedral there, before heading off to enjoy a lobster dinner in Fishguard. In 1953, he and Caitlin visited St David's, and while there posed for a photograph, possible the last of them together.

Also in 1953 he went to Llangollen, with Caitlin and Colm, to write about the International Eisteddfod for the BBC, and came to Tenby, yet another Welsh seaside town, to perform *Under Milk Wood* at the Salad Bowl café, almost certainly his last public performance on this side of the

Atlantic before his ill-fated final trip to the USA the following month.

The foregoing reminds me that there are many places in Wales, especially those away from the main sites associated with Dylan that I've still to visit. I would particularly like to spend more time in the Welsh countryside, which, although very similar to Ireland in its rolling hills and predominance of greens and browns, has the added advantage of not having suffered from the 'bungalow blight' that resulted from our recent massive building boom and poor planning laws. It impresses me that I can drive from Fishguard to Cardigan and see hardly any new houses under construction and ruining the beautiful landscape. I know from my Welsh friends that such tight application of planning laws has social implications, in that young buyers are priced out of the market. But while I would understand the call for a loosening of the planning regulations, I'd hoped it would be achieved without Wales suffering the same negative impact that has despoiled much of the Irish countryside beyond practical repair. Time will tell.

# Laugharne
# Dylan's Resting Place

Apart from his birthplace Swansea, the location most associated with Dylan Thomas is Laugharne, the quaint coastal village on the estuary of the River Taf facing Carmarthen Bay. It became his resting place, and some will argue that Laugharne was ultimately Dylan's spiritual home and since his death it's become a place of pilgrimage for Dylan admirers from all over the world. Indeed, because of the Dylan connection, Laugharne has been called the Stratford-Upon-Avon of Wales, in which I find an uncanny echo of his boyhood reference to 'Uplands on Avon' in that letter to Nancy referred to earlier. Laugharne's layout and general demeanour may have changed little since Dylan's days when it was populated by people of mixed descent, including Spanish, English and Dutch people intermingled with natives who spoke either English or Welsh or both.

Dylan fell in love with Laugharne in 1934 when visiting with his friend and writer Glyn Jones, and in a marvellous and eponymous piece for radio he referred to it as 'this timeless, beautiful, barmy (both spellings) town' adding that 'there is nowhere like it anywhere at all'. He described how, like others, he 'came one day for the day, and never left, got off the bus and forgot to get on again.' That may be a typical Dylanesque exaggeration, but it's also a convincing reflection of the affection he felt towards the town. He first came to Laugharne by ferry while on holidays as a boy in Llangain, and after he settled in Laugharne that same ferry service enabled Dylan to continue to make trips across to his friends across the estuary in the Llansteffan and Llangain area. On a visit to Ferryside I got a superb sense of the breadth of the estuary with its three rivers meeting, the reverse view, as it were, of the view from Laugharne.

Although I didn't get off the bus and forget to get back on, I too fell in love with Laugharne when I first arrived there by car in the mid-seventies. I was smitten by its sense of timelessness, of letting the rest of the world get on with its business while not paying too much attention to it. On King Street, although my memory might be playing tricks as to its precise location, I came upon a shop, possible a pharmacy, which had a poster in the window advertising an outing or a pilgrimage to somewhere foreign. The poster was sunburned and curling at the edges, and was several years out of date. Clearly, there was no rush to take it down, and maybe there were far more important things to do with one's time. I could imagine a similar scene in a rural Irish town, with the shop's proprietor thinking that the poster wasn't doing anybody any harm and sure maybe one day he'd get around to replacing it but in the meantime... It was almost like walking on to a film-set, such was the sense of almost-unreality I felt in Laugharne. On that visit myself and my companion found a guest house near The Grist, and on subsequent visits my wife and I stayed in a bed and breakfast close to St Martin's Church and graveyard.

When I was invited to deliver a talk at Rhos-y-Gilwen about the importance of culture in attracting tourists to Ireland, I argued that the same might be done for Wales. Mentioning some of the places I'd been drawn to and why, I quipped that I had brought two wives and one mother-in-law to Laugharne, although not at the same time! That first visit was with my first wife, but the later visits were with my second wife Mary, and on one occasion with Mary's mother Clare.

Caitlin first visited Laugharne with Augustus John in 1936 when she came to stay with the author Richard Hughes who, as we shall see shortly, was to be a good friend and supporter of both Dylan and Caitlin. Dylan, knowing she was here with John, actually followed her down with the help of Fred Janes and Fred's car. Much to John's disgust, Dylan and Caitlin ended up cuddling in the back of Janes' vehicle after it broke down, and some say that this was the start of their real relationship. If true, I think it most appropriate, since this was where they were to end their days together.

Laugharne seemed to provide an environment for Dylan that was most conducive to his engagement with his muse, as well as being the kind of seaside location he seemed to be most drawn to. The poem 'Into her lying down head' was begun in Laugharne. Another, 'The tombstone told', having been started in Swansea, was completed here. It was based on a story Dylan had heard about a Welsh bride who died while wearing her wedding dress. 'Poem in October', which he said was 'the first place poem I've written', is redolent of Laugharne. It's also a technically complex work, each verse composed to a strict syllable count that is traditional in Welsh verse. It also contains the phrase 'the castle brown as owls', a fine poetic description of the ivy-clad 700-year-old Laugharne Castle.

That castle is adjacent to Hughes' Castle House. The Thomases often stayed with Hughes and his wife Frances, attracted not least by Richard's impressive wine cellar which Dylan made full use of, not always with his host's full knowledge. Dylan was also allowed to use part of the house as a writing room, and this is where he composed some of the stories that formed part of *Portrait of The Artist As A Young Dog*. Around this time, Dylan took part in a one-act farce called *The Devil Among The Skins* which Hughes thought was not of the quality the people of Laugharne deserved.

After staying for a while over Easter with his parents in Bishopston, Dylan and Caitlin came to reside in Laugharne in May 1938, at first occupying a small fisherman's cottage called Eros in Gosport Street which Hughes had found for them. The house was only a few doors away from The Corporation Arms, and the local cockle factory was also close-by. The garden of their house led down to the muddy estuary, and they could see the cockle-pickers leading their donkeys back from the sands at Ginst Point.

Dylan called it a 'small, damp fisherman's furnished cottage', and its tiny rooms contained Victorian furniture which they both disliked intensely. George Tremlett wrote that the older townsfolk remembered them as the first hippies to arrive in West Wales. In Dylan's poem 'On no work of words' there's a phrase 'three lean months' that most likely refers to the trying times they endured while living at Eros. In an earlier draft he muses tellingly about 'no work done in summer Laugharne among the cockle boats and by the castle with the boatlike birds'.

After that difficult period they moved to another house in Laugharne. Compared to Eros, Sea View was a most imposing, tall building situated near the castle, and it provided them with far greater comfort than Eros. It also had the advantage of being close to the gazebo of the castle and to which Dylan could retire for the peace and quiet he seemed to need in order to write. Dylan and Caitlin started their family here, and the poem 'A saint about to fall' anticipates the arrival of their first child Llewelyn. The phrase 'his father's house in the sands' is most likely a reference to Sea View. Caitlin later described their spell in this house as 'their only happy time together'. While there they enjoyed visits from many friends, including Augustus John, who described it as looking like a doll's house. Mervyn Levy, Vernon Watkins, Henry Treece and others came too. But, sadly, their apparent idyll came to a premature end, when mounting debts with local suppliers required them to move away in 1940.

The hard-pressed couple could hardly have imagined during those straitened times that Laugharne would in time become their last home, and a place where Dylan was, arguably, at his most fulfilled. When Richard Hughes vacated Castle House there was some talk of Dylan wanting to buy it, but his finances were, as always, at a low ebb. Fortunately, and not for the first time, his great friend and benefactor Margaret Taylor came to his family's rescue. In an extraordinary act of generosity, and a sure sign of her boundless faith in Dylan's talents, she paid for a lease on a property in Laugharne known as The Boathouse so that Dylan and Caitlin could make it their family home. They moved into it in the spring of 1949, with their son Llewelyn having since been joined by their daughter Aeronwy, while their third and last child, Colm, was already on the way.

An appreciative Dylan once wrote to Taylor telling her that Laugharne was 'this place I love and where I want to live'. The Boathouse, which he graphically and memorably described as 'my seashaken house on a breakneck of rocks', is located right beside the estuary. It's built upon a rise, and, at high tide, the sea often dashes upon its garden wall and is known to have flooded the garden on occasion. It affords a splendid panoramic view out over the River Taf to the fields about Pentowin, with the wide estuary of mudflats and sandbanks, where the Taf meets two other rivers, the Towy and the Gwendraeth, spread out in front. Even if there were no connections with the poet, it's still a magical place, and I never tire of the walk along the seashore from the car park under the castle, or along the pathway at the back of the house where I've often enjoyed the magnificent views out over the estuary. The house itself was initially sparsely furnished, since the Thomas family did not have much in the way of material possessions, but it was cosy, with six small rooms plus a kitchen distributed over three storeys. During a 1975 visit, their son Colm wrote in the visitors' book, 'It used to be a good house to live in'. The dwelling latterly housed a desk which Dylan and his father used in 5 Cwmdonkin Drive, thereby completing a circle connecting the poet's early life to its end. More recently I've enjoyed the audio-visual display material that fleshes out relevant aspects of Dylan's life. The addition of a cafe area out the back, where you can sit and somehow feel the spirit of Dylan hovering about, encourages visitors to linger a while longer.

Aeronwy remembers her father testing extracts from *Under Milk Wood* by reading them aloud all over the house, and even when he was having one of his long baths. He would often interrupt Caitlin in the middle of her household chores to try out a fresh piece of writing and seek her opinion about it. In the mornings he often read and wrote letters in the house, but when it came to his 'real' work, Dylan escaped to his isolated writing shed at the back of the house, originally a garage believed to have been built to shelter the first motor-car in Laugharne.

He was doubtlessly inspired by the magnificent views afforded by the shed's two windows as they looked out across the estuary and what he called 'the heron-priested shore'. He often brought bread with him from the house to throw out to the birds through one of the windows. Occasionally his quiet would be interrupted by explosions from the nearby government munitions site, an important employment source for Laugharne which at that time lived mostly off fishing and farming. The shed itself was invariably untidy, with bits of newspapers and discarded fragments of poems scattered about the floor. When his friend Glyn Jones visited the shed he drew Dylan's attention to the place across the estuary where his own grandfather was born. Dylan claimed it was beside the Pentowin farm where *his* own grandfather was born. But I think the only real family connection he had with Pentowin was that his Uncle Jim and Aunt Annie had farmed it in the days before they moved to Fern Hill. In the same general direction, Dylan could see the church of Llanybri with its spires, 'the size of a snail with its horns through the mist.'

It's possible today to peer into a replica of the original shed on the same site, to see the room much as it might have looked in Dylan's days, with its stove, and pages of writing tossed haphazardly around the desk and floor, and photos and postcards stuck upon the wall. I've often looked in and easily imagined him toiling away at his desk, fag in hand, wrestling words into his immortal work and testing them aloud. To keep him safe from temptations and distractions, Caitlin often locked him in here for the afternoon, and the children were all warned to leave him alone to get on with his work.

'Poem on his Birthday', which he worked on painstakingly here, uses the phrase 'in his house on stilts', a phrase applicable to both The Boathouse and its shed. In one draft of that poem Dylan refers to the latter in the lines, 'In this estuary room, with Walt Whitman over my head'. Photos of DH Lawrence and WH Auden also once adorned the shed. He also put two reproductions of Botticelli's painting *The Birth Of Venus* on the walls, and the phrase 'naked Venus' appears in his poem 'My hero bares his nerves'.

The poem 'Over Sir John's hill' was inspired by the low hill of that name that can be seen to the right as one looks out from the shed across the estuary with its abundant birdlife, herons and cormorants, and what he called 'the dab-filled shallow'. The poem contains references to the myriad aspects of nature that were present in the landscape all around him, while also reflecting his more general thoughts on the natural cycle of life, death and renewal. The importance of this environment to Dylan's art may be gauged by the fact that this was probably his first new poem in two years.

On the other side of the hill is Salt House Farm whose name has its echoes in the Salt Lake Farm of *Under Milk Wood*. There's a drawing Dylan made of the layout of the imaginary Llaregub that looks like a mirror image of the view from this hill, suggesting Laugharne as the basis for the topography of the play. In support of the 'Laugharne as the model for Llaregub' argument, Dylan's biographer John Ackerman also points out that Manchester House, Rose Cottage and Bay View are all named houses in Laugharne that are also used in the play, although I've been told that the same map has been used to bolster the New Quay claim too!

As Daniel Jones wrote in his introduction to a book of Dylan's poems, 'The later poems of Dylan Thomas are full of reference to, or imagery derived from, the water-birds and the birds of prey he saw in such numbers from the window of the hut where he worked, overlooking the Laugharne estuary'. The natural environment around that estuary fed into his poem 'Prologue' too, and 'Lament' was also composed here.

But apart from the inspirational sights and sounds it afforded him, the shed had other advantages in that it gave Dylan a retreat from the hubbub of family life. His relationship with Caitlin was often tempestuous, and could be physically and verbally abusive on both sides, as both constantly battled their own demons and each other. Yet, their daughter Aeronwy recalled her childhood around Laugharne as being free and unrestrained, describing it as a 'wonderful adventure playground.' So while Dylan was at work in his shed, away from home or just socialising in the village, the children and their friends roamed about the open countryside and around the estuary. His children were another influence on his poetry. 'In Country Sleep' has a reference to Aeronwy with the lines 'Sleep, good, for ever, slow and deep, spelled rare and wise, My girl ranging the night in the rose and shire of the hobnail tales ...'

Dylan's shed backed onto the path, now called Dylan's Walk, where a neighbour recalled finding scraps of paper discarded on the ground. She tried, in vain, to piece it together again, leaving us all to wonder what it might have contained. Was it some mere trivial note, or the germ of a lost poem, perhaps? As I've walked that path in the past, I've often glanced down, foolishly hoping for a similar find. For Dylan, that path conveniently led to Cliff Road and Brown's Hotel, a favoured haunt of Dylan to which he sometimes walked two or three times a day, and where some of the best known photos of him were taken. On my last visit to the town I was disappointed to see the hotel closed and in obvious need of refurbishment. I had enjoyed several visits here to quaff a couple of brown ales and to wonder what impact Dylan's presence had on the locals. Were they aware of his literary importance? Did they care? I also wonder at my own habit, and one I share with countless others, of imagining that by being in a place associated with a great creative artist one is able to get closer to the artist and the work. I know there are many who think that such notions are mere fantasy, but I'm not convinced, and offer my own experience as evidence to the contrary.

Brown's was really a kind of home-from-home for Dylan, where he used to enjoy a game of cards and absorbed the local gossip supplied by his close friend Ivy Williams, co-owner of the pub with her husband Ebie. The Williamses understandably played a major role in Dylan's Laugharne life, as, apart from Brown's, they also ran the local taxi and bus services. Ivy was extremely generous to Dylan whenever he was short of money, which was often. Caitlin described her as Dylan's 'substitute mother' for whom, Caitlin claimed, he had a deeper love than his real mother. If while socialising in Brown's, Dylan's ears caught a telling phrase, or he was struck by a useful idea, he would jot it down on any convenient piece of paper for later consideration. When he made his first solo appearance on BBC television, it was in Brown's that Caitlin watched it. It was part of a series called *Speaking Personally*, and Dylan's contribution was broadcast from St Asaph Cathedral in North Wales.

Dylan also drank in the Corporation Arms, which has also been suggested as the basis for the Sailors Arms in *Under Milk Wood*. He visited the Cross House Inn on the square they call the Grist, some of whose regulars are also believed to have influenced the characters Dylan created for the play. Dylan refers to the Grist in a letter to his father, in which he expressed his appalled reaction to the War, writing that 'wives and mothers weep around the stunted memorial in the Grist'.

Despite other towns claiming to be the prototype for Llareggub, Dylan himself once tellingly said 'What Laugharne really needs is a play about well-known Laugharne characters'. When *Under Milk Wood* first emerged, many Laugharne people were hurt by what they felt was a lampooning of their town and its inhabitants, but later most of them grew to like it, and even argued proudly over who had inspired this or that particular character.

Between the Corporation Arms and the Cross House Inn stood the Town Hall with its clock tower, said to be the origin of the reference 'as tall as the town clock-tower' in the play. Close to Brown's is Corran Books, owned by George Tremlett who was an ardent admirer of Dylan. George wrote books about Dylan and Caitlin, and argued that Dylan was the first rock star. I rarely visit Laugharne without visiting the premises which once seemed to stretch forever up and down and out the back, with rooms full of books and old magazines, including copies of the music papers I used to eagerly devour in the seventies.

In 1949, Dylan's parents moved to a house in Laugharne called The Pelican, the ground floor flat of which Dylan rented for them. It was in King Street opposite Browne's Hotel. Not surprisingly, Dylan was an almost daily visitor to the house where he would regularly do *The Times* crossword with his father. It was DJ's loss of eyesight and his general decline that inspired what is probably Dylan's greatest poem 'Do not go gentle into that good night'. In a letter to the publisher who first printed this poem he tenderly wrote 'The only person I can't show the little enclosed poem to is, of course, my father, who doesn't know he's dying'. When he read the poem at the University of Utah he introduced it by mentioning his father's atheism, but acknowledged how he'd grown soft and gentle at the last. Dylan's father eventually died in The Pelican in 1952, and his passing inspired Dylan to write 'Elegy', an unfinished poem about DJ's death. Dylan took his father's death very badly, and some have even suggested that it hastened his own passing. His sister Nancy died soon too, of cancer in Bombay, coincidentally on the same day in 1953 that Dylan set off for his third American tour.

Ominously, that same year Dylan was invited to give a poetry reading in Lampeter, and wrote in reply demanding a fee of five guineas, plus expenses. He complimented the organisers for their forward planning, but in a reference to the planned date of the recital, he ended his letter with the words, 'if we're not all dead by then.' Tragically, as fate would have it, he was, and it was not long before Dylan's mother was the only member of the family still alive.

Dylan died on November 9th 1953 in New York, during the fourth of his momentous poetry reading tours of the USA that had begun the previous month. It was only a year after his father's death and he was thirty-nine years young. Although the death certificate famously attributed his demise to 'an insult to the brain', others have variously put it down to the dimming of his poetic talent, money worries, troubles in his marriage, the pressures of the American tours, his habitual drinking, or the drugs he was given to help him deal with his ill health, which may or may not have included undiagnosed diabetes. Maybe it was all of those, or maybe none. We'll probably never know for certain.

Just before he left for that fateful trip he recorded a radio piece about Laugharne, and it was broadcast while he lay dying in hospital on the other side of the Atlantic. On its journey from New York by ship, his coffin was collected from Southampton dock by Ebie Williams, and his body was laid out in The Pelican because it was far more accessible for family and other mourners than the Boathouse.

The poet is buried in the peaceful graveyard of the thirteenth century St Martin's Church, on the road heading out of Laugharne towards St Clears. Local rumour says that during the funeral The Boathouse was burgled and that valuable documents and manuscripts were stolen. Even today, there is much speculation in Laugharne as to the identity of the opportunistic thieves and the location of the stolen goods.

Caitlin complained that he should have been buried in the old section of the graveyard, instead of the modern part, and she also expressed her desire for his remains to be re-interred at the Boathouse. This request has not been met, and seems unlikely to be. After the funeral, Caitlin supposedly threatened to kill herself by jumping off a nearby cliff, and there were also rumours of her wanting to throw herself into the open grave. Caitlin, who died in 1994, now lies in the same grave, their joint resting place marked by a modest white wooden cross that reflects the physical simplicity of their lives. He'd once said, 'When I'm dead I want to be buried and to feel the violets growing over me'.

Over the years since his premature demise, the name of Dylan Thomas has spawned a worldwide industry of its own. Not much more than a decade after his passing, his status as a writer was acknowledged by The Beatles when they included his photograph among the international luminaries who featured on the famous cover of their groundbreaking album *Sgt. Pepper's Lonely Hearts Club Band.* Artists as varied as the London singer-songwriter Ralph McTell and the Scot Robin Williamson have written and recorded songs inspired by his life and work. Rock legends such as John Lennon, Van Morrison and other cultural icons have cited him as a profound influence.

A great enthusiast for convivial conversation, Dylan was also somewhat of a showman, both in social situations and professionally on radio and on the stage. He left a substantial treasury of recordings that prove him to have been an engaging performer of his own works, as well as those of other writers, on both sides of the Atlantic and through more than 200 broadcasts on radio. Those broadcasts included readings of the works of several other Welsh poets that he admired, including Idris Davies, Alun Lewis, Vernon Watkins, George Herbert and Glyn Jones. He read an abridged, serialised version of *Autobiography of A Super-tramp* written by the Newport novelist WH Davies. In an article for *The Herald of Wales*, published under the heading 'The Poets of Swansea' he described him as the most talented Welsh writer then writing in English. There's also a recording of him reading 'The Traveller's Curse After Misdirection', composed by Robert Graves having been translated from the Welsh.

Dylan participated in many discussions, including one broadcast from Swansea that included friends like Daniel Jones, Vernon Watkins, Alfred Janes and John Prichard. Apart from those names already mentioned, he generously worked at popularising such Welsh writers as Gwyn Jones, RS Thomas and Gwyn Thomas in direct contradiction of suggestions that he had turned his back on the talents of his native country.

In the introduction to his 2003 biography *Dylan Thomas – A New Life*, Andrew Lycett records that a Google search of the phrase 'do not go gentle into that good night' produced 21,000 hits. A similar search in 2010 came up with over 6.5 million. This is an extraordinary achievement in a world allegedly disinterested in such non-material matters as poetry and literary works. It offers ample proof that the work of this great Welsh writer continues to spread throughout the world.

As time passes, greater numbers are attracted to the art, the artist, the man, his life and the aspects of Wales and the Welsh that inspired one of the greatest poets of the 20th century, Dylan Marlais Thomas, the bard of Cwmdonkin Drive, Swansea, Wales.

# More About
# the Man

# An Exclusive Interview with Frank Jenkins

I was delighted in 2011, while on a visit to Carmarthen town, to be introduced by my Ceredigion friends Richard and Wyn Jones to Frank Jenkins. Initially our contact was simply because Frank is a musician of note in the locality and the Joneses assumed, rightly, that we would have lots to talk about. But I found we had other mutual interests when Frank told me he'd lived in Laugharne. Not only that, but he'd he gone to school with Aeronwy Thomas and also, as a very young boy, known Dylan Thomas! Better still, his father's fish and chip van had been written about by Dylan!

To me, meeting somebody as affable as Frank who clearly knew the Thomas family while they lived in Laugharne was a real find. So, next time we met I told Frank about this book and he willingly agreed to be interviewed for it. I was amazed that this was the first time he'd talked to anybody in the media at length about his days in Laugharne when his neighbours included Dylan Thomas.

Born in 1942, Frank Jenkins is one of the few living Welshman who not only knew Dylan Thomas while they both lived in Laugharne, but he went to the local school in King Street with Dylan's only daughter Aeronwy. In fact, they shared the same class for a while from when Frank was aged about six. He also played with her and her friends in and around the Boathouse where the Thomas family lived and where he often met Dylan himself.

He'd numerous other opportunities to observe the great man at first hand, because his childhood home in 13 Victoria Street was directly along Dylan's path as he made his regular pilgrimages from the Boathouse to Brown's Hotel or to visit other parts of the seaside village. Frank admits seeing Dylan 'a lot' in those days. 'I can remember him from the time when I was about five or six years of age. I can still recall this fairly solid figure with a mop of brown curly hair. He often wore a pair of corduroy trousers, a jacket and shirt and a pair of think crepe-soled shoes. Sometimes he'd have a tie in place of a belt for his trousers. That's the image that comes to mind whenever I think of him, but to us he was just like the other men of his age in Laugharne.'

Of course the people in the town knew that Dylan was a poet, but, as Frank explains, 'We didn't realise that he was making a living out of it, or that he was becoming so famous, but obviously he was. Not a lot of people listened much to the radio in those days, so we never really heard any of his poetry until much later.'

But there's one of Dylan's poems that stands out in

Frank's mind. 'He wrote this poem called "Laugharne" which mentions a fish and chip van that was a converted Rolls Royce! That fish and chip van belonged to my father, Arthur Jenkins. It had the back section removed in order to convert it. He used to keep the van parked outside a house in Orchard Park we moved to after we vacated Victoria Street. Dylan probably saw it all over the place, because my father had a regular route he used to go round, and locals would know what time to expect him at different places like the Grist or outside certain pubs. He had a big klaxon horn he's sound off to let people know he'd arrived, a bit like the Mr Whippy icecream vans of later years. You could hear my dads's klaxon for miles! I'd be very surprised if Dylan didn't buy some fish and chips from my dad because nearly everybody did. From what I can remember, the cheapest price was three pence in old money for the smallest bag. One guy ordered eighty bags from him at Pendine!'

Frank was too young to be allowed into Brown's Hotel. 'But we'd often see Dylan and his wife Caitlin walking along the street with their dog Mably. I was usually wary of Mably because he could be vicious if he was in a bad mood, but I thought Mrs Thomas was a lovely person,' he recalls.

He also remembers Aeronwy very well. 'We used to call her Aeron and we played a lot around the Boathouse and generally around Laugharne with the other kids, especially in the afternoons after school and during the summer holidays. She was just like the rest of us, getting up to a little harmless mischief like we all did. Her brother Llewelyn used to play with us too, sometimes, but he was a bit older than us. But Colm was just a baby at the time. I spent a lot of time in the Boathouse as a young boy. Of course we had no way of knowing how famous it would be later, with people travelling from all over the world to visit it now. They had a small rowing boat called *The Cuckoo*. One day it was parked on the mud flats below the house because the tide was out. Aeron and I and a friend called Clive Mosely got into it and Mrs Thomas rowed us out in it. For us, that was a big adventure at that age! It was a great place for any child to grow up, even though most families had no television or radio, we had the fields and the estuary to play in.'

He can especially recall cherries. As he told me, 'It was shortly after the war when it wasn't as easy to buy sweets and fruit as it is today with shops everywhere and more money around. But I remember the Thomases always seemed to have a big bowl of fresh red cherries. Caitlin would day, "here you are, boys and girls, help yourselves, but don't swallow the stones." They were a real treat and a bit of a luxury at a time when ration books were still in use for most basic goods. You were lucky if you could buy one or two apples or one or two plums then. So having cherries was a bit posh by comparison to what most folks could have,' he reckons.

That said, he reckons there was little that was posh about the Boathouse itself. 'It was just an ordinary house to us kids, no different from any other house we went into. Some people have said the house would be a bit untidy, but that was not my experience. It was a relaxed, homely place. But the Thomases stood out in the town because they had regular visitors from places in England that none of us knew. I don't remember Dylan mixing much with the local dignitaries. I think he preferred to mix with ordinary people like my father.'

Dylan's writing shed was off-limits to everybody, including his own children, so Frank's contact with the family was invariably confined to the house itself and the surrounding fields and estuary, while playing with Aeron and their pals. 'But if he came upon us in the house he would always be very friendly and say hello to us. He wasn't a man to make a big fuss of kids, as far as I could see, but he was always pleasant and good-humoured anytime I was there', says Frank.

When news of Dylan's death filtered back to Laugharne, Frank was living in Upton House, a three-storey house not far from St Martin's Church and graveyard. 'People were obviously shocked that he died so young. A lot of people came from all over Wales and outside for the funeral, so Laugharne was crowded. His body was brought home to his parents' house Pelican, and they had to get the coffin out through the window.'

Frank left Laugharne in 1966 aged twenty-four, by which time the dead Dylan was a worldwide celebrity poet and beginning to be accepted broadly in Laugharne as a major literary figure. 'My parents still lived in Laugharne and they told me about the steady increase in visitors that were coming there because of Dylan, especially Americans who up to then had been a rarity around this part of Wales. I think they were often surprised by the modesty of the cross around his grave. I think they expected a massive structure of some kind. Some of them even offered to buy the Rolls Royce chip van from my father because it had been mentioned in Dylan's poem! Unfortunately it was long gone for scrap. But it still lives on in my memory and in the poem. To this day I can remember its number. YE7615,' he says.

# Dylan's Welsh Friends

Dylan's attraction to pubs was not just about the beer and the smoking. He had a big appetite for convivial company, for friends with whom he could gossip and banter and swap philosophical notions about a wide range of topics, whether they be serious, trivial or totally fanciful. He had a sharp tongue, a quick wit, a masterful facility with words and a finely-developed sense of humour, and was as likely to use that humour to puncture his own pomposity as that of others.

Central to Dylan's development as a young artist were the many friends, co-workers and collaborators from various arts disciplines who formed The Kardomah Gang, (also often referred to as the Kardomah Boys or Kardomah Set). That was the name tagged onto the irregular collection of poets, artists and musicians who used to gather at the original Kardomah Café when it was located in Castle Street in Swansea in the 1930s. The Kardomah back then contained two separate sections. In one would gather the middle-aged hoi polloi from the locality, while the upstairs area would be mainly occupied by the younger set. The most notable member of this gang was Dylan, but he was not the only one to enjoy a successful career in later years. It could be argued that the passing of time has exaggerated the gang's membership into a kind of organised cross-cultural movement. It would be far closer to reality to regard them as a disparate group who met whenever it suited them, and whose numbers varied haphazardly from time to time. In a sense they have collectively been portrayed with the same inaccuracy as the 'Angry Young Men', the British playwrights and novelists of the mid-fifties who were lazily gathered together under a flag of convenience as if they had wilfully joined forces in one movement. In truth, most of the so-called angry young men denied membership of this contrived collective. That is not to say that the Swansea Gang members of that earlier time did not act as a stimulus on each other. Far from it. At the cafe they would drink coffee and talk frenziedly about all manner of subjects, including, as Dylan himself put it, 'Einstein and Epstein, Stravinsky and Greta Garbo, death and religion, Picasso and girls'.

The gang's fluid membership included such notables as Daniel Jones, Vernon Watkins, Alfred Janes, Mervyn Levy and John Prichard, among several others. Depending on whose account you pay heed to, the gang could also include Tom Warner, later to become a serious composer. It was Daniel Jones who introduced Dylan to the French horn-playing Warner who was the son of an English vicar and who also resided in the Uplands near Dylan's home. Another floating member was Mabley Owen, whom another member Charlie Fisher once described as the most amusing talker he'd ever heard. Owen was a keen drinker and a witty man. Keidrych Rees was another erstwhile member of the Kardomah Gang, and he edited the magazine *Wales*. The gang was virtually all-male, despite the admission that girls were often high on their agenda as a subject for discussion, although they were sometimes joined by Evelyn (Titch) Philips and her sister Vera. The latter was later to feature in Dylan's adventures in New Quay when her husband fired shots at the bungalow Dylan was staying in.

Dylan, who liked the challenge and variety afforded by creative collaborations, composed works with Watkins and Jones among others. Jones, Janes, Fisher and Watkins all show up with the author in *Return Journey* and linked to their as yet unfulfilled ambitions. The BBC in 1949 recorded a radio programme that included Dylan, Jones, Watkins, Janes and John Prichard, and they were later the subject of a tv programme called *Kardomah Boys* broadcast by BBC Wales in 1997.

Sadly, the original Kardomah no longer exists. Over three nights in 1941, Swansea suffered intense bombing by the German Luftwaffe. Castle Street was badly hit, and many buildings, including several shops and the Kardomah, were reduced to ruin. Dylan wrote about the destruction in his radio play *Return Journey to Swansea* in which he describes the Kardomah as being 'razed to the snow'. After the end of the war, the café relocated to nearby Portland Street where it remains to this day, a magnet for tourists on the Dylan Thomas trail, many of whom are not aware that it is not the original location. Incidentally, the decision to ban smoking in 2004 in the new Kardomah, as in all other cafés and restaurants in Wales, would hardly have met with his approval, especially since he used to enjoy a cigarette or two anywhere he went.

There were many Welsh friends and supporters of Dylan who were not fully-paid-up members of the Kardomah crowd, including the BBC producer Aneirin Talfan Davies, his journalist colleague Freddie Farr, broadcaster Wynford Vaughan-Thomas and the actor Richard Burton. Their number, as well as the tenacity of loyal friendships which often lasted through nearly all of Dylan's life, show once again how important Wales and the Welsh were to him.

### Richard Burton

Internationally-acclaimed Welsh actor became as famous for his various marriages to, and bust-ups with, actress Elizabeth Taylor as he did for his fine work on film, stage and record. He was an occasional drinking buddy of Dylan's, and was particularly fond of recalling a session with Dylan and the Irish poet Louis MacNeice at which Dylan encouraged them to recite their favourite poems. It was quite appropriate that Burton took on the role of First Voice in both the BBC recording of *Under Milk Wood* in 1954 and the 1971 film version, the same part Dylan had spoken during the play's initial New York performances. Their voices have a similar resonance and depth, and give full value to every syllable. Burton had a deep, mellifluous and sombre voice redolent of the Welsh valleys. They had worked together in 1946 on the BBC production of the play *In Parenthesis* by David Jones, and the actor told how Dylan declaimed the words 'Mam, Mam' so loudly that the other actors thought it extraordinary.

Burton was born Richard Jenkins, one of thirteen children, in 1925 in the village of Pontrhydyfen, near Port Talbot in Wales, and he first came to the attention of theatre fans and critics with his stage role in *The Lady's Not for Burning* in London in 1949, followed by a stint on Broadway the following year. His first Hollywood screen part was in *My Cousin Rachel* in 1952, and he enjoyed a high-profile affair with Taylor during the filming of *Cleopatra* in 1963. He also starred in *The Spy Who Came in from the Cold*, *Who's Afraid of Virginia Woolf?* and *Equus*. He earned much acclaim on Broadway in *Camelot* in 1960 and *Hamlet* in 1964. He and Taylor starred together in many films as their celebratory and gossip status soared. She won several Oscars, but although he was nominated several times, including for his role in *Who's Afraid of Virginia Woolf?*, Burton never won. He also impressed rock music fans with his speaking role in Jeff Wayne's *War of the Worlds* concept album in the seventies.

But it was his tempestuous relationship with Taylor that turned him into a living legend. They married in 1964 after she divorced actor Eddie Fisher. The uproar provoked by their relationship prompted the US State Department to ask to have his visa revoked as they deemed him 'detrimental to the morals of the youth.' Burton was an intemperate alcoholic, a factor that partly led to the couple's divorce in 1974. In 1975 they remarried, and divorced again in 1976. Burton later wed ex-model Suzy Hunt and then Sally Hay.

Apart from his issues with alcohol, Burton also suffered from painful spinal problems and underwent neck surgery. He died suddenly of a cerebral haemorrhage in Switzerland in 1984.


**Aneirin Talfan Davies**
Davies was born in 1909 and became a poet, a noted broadcaster and a respected literary critic. He was raised in Gorseinon, about six miles north-west of Swansea. In the 1930s he was employed in London as a pharmacist, but he was eventually to settle back in Swansea. He was appointed Head of Programmes for BBC Wales and was the producer of programmes that included Dylan's works. He was an enthusiastic supporter of Dylan, and argued with his bosses in London to broadcast Dylan's *Quite Early One Morning*. In 1951 he was also responsible for having Dylan broadcast from the Festival of Britain in order to bring a Welsh perspective. During the last few days of his life Dylan

travelled from Laugharne to Swansea to record for the BBC his thoughts on Laugharne at Davies' request. After Dylan died, Davies penned a critical study of Dylan as a religious poet. He even believed that Dylan was considering converting to Roman Catholicism not long before he died, although there's little or no evidence in support of this claim.

With his brother Alun Talfan Davies, Aneirin set up the publishing company Llyfrau'r Dryw. He was also known by his bardic name Aneurin ap Talfan and established the Welsh language magazines *Heddiw* (meaning 'today' and *Barn* (Welsh for 'opinion'). He translated the poems of Christina Rossetti into Welsh and contributed anonymous satirical pieces to the *Western Mail* under the pseudonym Theomemphus. He was a devout Anglican, and his writings were redolent of Christian themes. Davies died in 1980.


**Freddie Farr**

Farr and Dylan worked together on the same Swansea newspaper the *South Wales Evening Post*, and during that time the more streetwise Farr served as a sort of role-model for Dylan, introducing him to the delights of many of Swansea's pubs, such as The Three Lamps on Temple Street. He was quick-witted and untidy, the image of the archetypal newshound as depicted in countless movies on the big screen. He encouraged Dylan in the finer points of the reporter's profession, including how to maximise one's expense claims. It helped that one of his jobs at the newspaper was passing expense claims submitted by the journalistic staff. Their shared experiences around The Strand area of Swansea fed into Dylan's story 'Old Garbo'. Farr was a boxing enthusiast and had picked up the nickname 'Half-Hook', and under both names he is mentioned in *Quite Early One Morning*.

## Charles Fisher

Generally known as Charlie, Fisher was a journalist and writer, and the last of the Kardomah gang to die. He initially got to know Dylan when they were classmates at Swansea Grammar School, where he played the part of Thomas's stage wife in John Galsworthy's play *Strife*. He admitted to being a totally unruly pupil, and said that while at the school he learned some English from Dylan's father DJ, but little else. He summed DJ up as a teacher who loved English, but hated boys.

He and Dylan worked together as reporters on the local *Evening Post* newspaper. Fisher himself said 'The Kardomah was important to us both as a place to report to and a place to find out what was going on. It was our touchstone. Good talk and good coffee. Well, very ordinary coffee.' Here, Fisher listened as Dylan recited early drafts of his poems out loud. In a letter to Fisher in the mid-thirties Dylan explained his laborious, if messy, method of writing his drafts of poems on both sides of sheets of scrap paper.

Fisher's early ambition was to be a classical concert pianist, and in that endeavour he listed his idols as Cortot, Lamond, Smeterlin and Schnabel. Of course, he would liked to have played as well as they did, but frankly admitted that he didn't have the talent, and even questioned whether he would have had the ability to withstand the pressure that goes with the job of concert performer.

Fisher served in the army on the Somerset coast and in France. He loved Paris in particular, and attended *Courses de Civilisation* at the Sorbonne, studying the French philosophers, writers and painters. Baudelaire, Teilhard de Chardin, James Fraser and Spengler were all important to him. He had his own poems published in literary magazines, and some believed he had as much poetic promise as Dylan. His poetry collection *The Locust Years* was published in the eighties, and he scripted talks and wrote two plays for BBC radio. When Dylan sought a partner-writer for his satirical novel *Death of the King's Canary* he started working with Fisher, but the collaboration came to nothing. When the war was over Fisher worked as a correspondent for Reuters at the British Parliament. He courted the singer Eartha Kitt, but married the Spanish opera singer Isabel Alonzo. In 1953 he moved to Canada and worked on the Canadian parliament's Hansard. He travelled widely, including the Far East, India, Mexico, Morocco, much of Europe, China, several islands in the Pacific, America (north and south), the Caribbean and India. In Thailand he studied the local dancing and taught English. He also lived among the gypsies in Granada for several years, experiences he recounted in his book *Adios Granada*. While in Spain, he played flamenco guitar to tourists. He died in 2006.

## Richard Hughes

Hughes, the author of the 1929 novel *A High Wind In Jamaica*, was born in Surrey in 1900, but had what Paul Ferris described as 'deep Welsh roots'. His mother Louise entertained the young boy with tales that sparked his imagination, especially those about Jamaica where she had lived until she was ten years old. Even before he could write, Hughes' fertile imagination was creating his own fictions and poems, reciting them for Louise to write down.

Hughes studied at Oriel College in Oxford, sharing company with other talented writers such as Aldous Huxley, Robert Graves, and TE Lawrence. *A High Wind in Jamaica* told the story of a group of children captured by pirates on their way to England. His depiction of children and childhood in the novel is believed to have helped lessen the sentimental, and often twee, view of childhood that had become commonplace in Victorian writings. Its success gained Hughes literary fame, as well as considerable popularity, not always comfortable bedfellows.

Hughes earned a considerable reputation for his plays too. He was the author of the first original play, entitled *Danger*, broadcast on BBC radio in 1924, and he was also to help Dylan get work from that august institution. A generous man, he was of great assistance to Dylan on many levels, not least in allowing him and Caitlin to stay in his bramble-and-ivy clad house beside the castle in Laugharne before they found a place of their own to live in. Like Dylan, he had also developed a great love of the sea.

Hughes was involved in early discussions with Dylan and Bert Trick about a work based on a Welsh town, the genesis of Llaregub that was eventually to underpin *Under Milk Wood*. He claimed to have suggested the title for *Portrait Of The Artist As A Young Dog*, but while that may be of little significance either way, it is indisputable that he played a crucial role in Dylan discovering the charms of Laugharne before choosing to spend the rest of his life there.

Despite being a fine writer, Hughes was not overly fond of the discipline required to get the work down on paper, preferring to go sailing or travel abroad as the fancy took him. A major share of his earnings from his seafaring novel *In Hazard*, which was mostly written in Laugharne, was spent making the house more habitable than he had found it. In fact, in order to bring in the money he needed for its upkeep he often took on more writing commissions than he could comfortably deliver.

He and his wife Frances, a painter, were regarded as the most generous of hosts, allowing visitors to stay even though they would distract the author from his writing duties. In 1938 Dylan had written to him asking if he and Caitlin could stop over with them while they looked for a more permanent place in the Laugharne area, so he invited them to stay with him in Laugharne free of charge. While Frances described Dylan as 'one of the most vivid and alive men she'd seen in years', Richard seemed to have a low opinion of Caitlin, and she didn't like him much either. But her reservations did not prevent her aiding Dylan's overindulgence in Hughes' impressive wine collection, and they both eagerly accepted the hospitality and excellent dining on offer from their hosts. When Dylan later discovered that Hughes was planning to leave Laugharne, he tried to lease their house, but, even with his benefactor Margaret Taylor's financial help and negotiation skills, he couldn't raise the necessary rent.

All told, Hughes authored four novels, several plays, poems, and children's stories. He died in Moredrin in Wales in April, 1976.

## Fred Janes

Alfred George Janes was born in Swansea in 1911. Before he grew to become a painter highly regarded for his originality, he attended Swansea Grammar School, where he and the younger Dylan first met, as well as Swansea College of Art. In 1931 he was awarded a scholarship to the Royal Academy in London, but left without completing his studies. He was a quietly independent man who was sympathetic to Dylan's literary ambitions from the days of their first meetings at the Kardomah and at Ralph's bookshop.

Janes shared a room in Fulham in London with Dylan after they were driven to the capital by Fred's father. The arrangement was not much to Dylan's liking, and he complained about the mess that included poems, more poems and canvasses. In 1934 Janes painted a much-reprinted portrait of Dylan that was initially exhibited at the Everyman Theatre in Hampstead, and later hung in the National Museum of Wales. He also painted a portrait of Mervyn Levy with whom the pair moved to another equally-unprepossessing London flat.

In 1936 Janes came back to live in Swansea for a time. He became a part-time teacher at Swansea College of Art and painted still lifes. Echoing Dylan's painstaking work method with his poems, Janes painted very slowly and with remarkable attention to detail, each piece worked on for many hours each day for months. In a letter to Vernon Watkins, Dylan impishly enquired, 'How is that blizzardly painter, that lightning artist, that prodigal canvas stacker?'

Author George Tremlett said that Janes (and Mervyn Levy) cast doubt on Dylan's allegedly prodigious capacity for drink. Nor did Janes share Dylan's determination to avoid the war, and enlisted in the Army soon after the war started, although poor eyesight restricted him to non-combatancy. He was transferred to Egypt to work in a prisoner-of-war camp. He learned to speak Swahili and Italian, and became an enthusiastic Italophile. In 1940 he married Mary Ross, a member of the Swansea Little Theatre.

Back in Swansea after the war he painted much-admired portraits of Daniel Jones and Vernon Watkins. In 1953 he and his family moved to a manor on the Gower Peninsula. In 1963 he took up a post at Croydon School of Art in London, enjoying the great pleasures of teaching, painting and the city. He was also very fond of music, which he thought of as closely allied to his own chosen discipline.

He was an unassuming and inoffensive man, much liked by his friends and students. He died in London in 1999.

## Augustus John

Augustus Edwin John was born in Tenby in Pembrokeshire in 1878. Having inherited a love of drawing and painting from his mother, he attended the Tenby School of Art and then the Slade School in London, the latter with his equally talented sister Gwen. An injury received while diving into the sea off the coast of Pembrokeshire during a holiday when he was about nineteen seemed to change his personality, and his painting became less restricted. He began to live a flamboyant Bohemian lifestyle, very unconventional for those conservative times, including for a while living in a caravan with gypsies. As his reputation as a painter soared, he received the prestigious Slade Prize in 1898 and came to be regarded as the most important British painter of his day.

In the First World War he joined the Canadian Army and was allowed to paint scenes on the Western Front. He was the only officer among Allied troops allowed to wear a beard, but he was sent home in disgrace for brawling, although he was subsequently allowed back. He was present at the Versailles Peace Conference in 1919 and painted portraits of some of the delegates there.

John was close to Caitlin Macnamara's family, and he allowed them to stay in his English residence after her father had left the family. He painted her, both clothed and otherwise. They had an affair, and she later implied that his sexual advances were not always welcome. Indeed, there were later suggestions that John forced himself on several of his models. He was more than thirty years older than Caitlin who fell in love with his son Caspar, who was (only) a decade older than her, but in her mid-teens she ran away with Vivienne John to become a dancer. After she had met Dylan in London, she and John were still carrying on a relationship, and in 1936, when they went to Laugharne to visit Richard Hughes, Dylan followed them. He had persuaded Fred Janes to drive him there on the pretext of going to the eisteddfod in Pembrokeshire. During that visit Dylan's open courting of Caitlin, and her equally open and positive responses, upset John to the extent that a physical altercation between the poet and the painter ensued.

Dylan's father DJ thought Caitlin was John's niece. But while John and Dylan had many verbal spats, and Dylan parodied him as the character Hercules Jones in the novel *The Death Of The King's Canary* he wrote with John Davenport, they remained friends. John visited Dylan in Laugharne, and did several well-known portraits of Dylan, including the frontispiece for Dylan's collection *The Map of Love*. He also painted such prominent figures as Thomas Hardy, George Bernard Shaw and TE Lawrence.

John published two books of autobiography, *Chiaroscuro* (1952) and *Finishing Touches* (1964). He passed away in 1961.

## Dan Jones

Born Daniel Jenkyn Jones in 1912, Dan Jones became a highly-regarded musician, one of the most revered Welsh composers and a noted linguist. He first befriended Dylan at Swansea Grammar School, and their friendship lasted, enduring some gaps, until Dylan's death.

Their first encounter, when Dylan was about fourteen, is recalled in Dylan's short story 'The Fight'. Jones claimed to have written seven novels before he even reached his teens, and played the violin and piano. Dylan often visited the Jones' home, a big semi-detached house in Sketty, where he would have found a relaxed and happy family, as well as lots of bustle and noise. It was there as boys that they collaborated on many artistic ventures, writing poems, songs and operas, 'broadcasting' an imaginary radio station, and publishing a journal called *The Era*.

Jones was aware of, and shared, Dylan's love of words and the belief that the sounds they made were often more important than their mere meanings. Dylan thought of him as clever, but felt his mind was too easily diverted into different disciplines when it might have been better had those talents and energies been channelled in a more specific, singular direction.

When Dylan and Caitlin were in America in 1952 Dylan sent a postcard to his friend depicting an ancient monument in Arizona. On the back of it he wrote a mocking epitaph of himself and Caitlin who were 'killed in action, Manhattan Island'. When Dylan died, Jones assumed responsibility for the funeral arrangements. He went with Ebie Williams to receive Dylan's coffin off the boat from New York at Southampton and take it back to The Pelican in Laugharne.

Jones had studied at the University of Wales and the Royal Academy of Music, and a Mendelssohn Travelling Scholarship enabled him to study in Czechoslovakia, France, Germany and Holland. During the Second World War he worked as a cryptographer, and decoded messages and documents in Romanian, Russian and Japanese at the famous Bletchley Park.

Charlie Fisher believed that Jones never received the fame his talent merited. In a creative life as prolific as Dylan's, he composed thirteen symphonies, the fourth of which he dedicated to Dylan, as well as string quartets, works for orchestra and choirs, and some operas. He also wrote the music for the premiere radio production of *Under Milk Wood* in 1954. He edited a volume of Dylan's prose pieces *A Prospect of the Sea* and the 1971 publication of *Dylan Thomas: The Poems.* His biography *My Friend Dylan Thomas* was published in 1977. Apart from Dylan, he maintained lengthy friendships with other Welsh artists, including Vernon Watkins and Ceri Richards. He was awarded an OBE in 1968, and died in 1993.

### Glyn Jones

Glyn Jones was a writer who was born in Merthyr Tydfil in 1905. Older than Dylan, their first contact seems to have been via a letter he wrote to the poet after Dylan's poem 'The Woman Speaks' had been published in *Adelphi* magazine in 1934. From there they became friends, and their respective family backgrounds had much in common. Jones later became one more Welsh artist to have stayed with Dylan in London. They went together to Laugharne in 1934 on what was probably Dylan's first visit to the seaside town, and they visited Caradoc Evans in Aberystwyth. Dylan described Jones as 'a nice, handsome young man with no vices', and it can be reasonably assumed that Dylan enjoyed his company. Like Dylan, he abhorred war, and he became a conscientious objector in 1940.

Jones lived in Swansea and worked as a schoolteacher in Cardiff. After he had his own poems published, he felt that Dylan saw him as a sort of benign threat, as if the latter wanted to be only Welsh poet from Swansea, somebody unique. This notion, even if true, does not explain why Dylan advised him to write short stories, as he could be just as much a rival in that genre as in poetry. Irrespective of the motivation behind Dylan's advice, Jones took it and published his stories, including the 1937 collection *The Blue Bed*. He observed how Dylan was fascinated by words, remembering that when he once used the word 'huddled' Dylan was so taken with it that he kept repeating it, enjoying the sound it made. They exchanged letters too, and Dylan wrote to him in 1935 telling him that he had to return to the country to work on his poetry.

While Dylan was living in Laugharne, Jones visited

him in 1949 with an idea for a BBC radio programme to be called *How I Write*, although the programme was never made. On that occasion, he was surprised to see how Dylan's appearance and health seemed to have deteriorated since he'd seen him last. In 1968 he published a book of biographical writings and included a piece about Dylan in it. He was an important figure in Anglo-Welsh literature and was appointed President of the Welsh Academy's English-language section. He died in 1995.

**Mervyn Levy**

The artist, writer, teacher and critic Mervyn Montague Levy was born in Swansea in the same year as Dylan. He attended Mrs Hole's school in Mirador Crescent in Swansea around the same time Dylan did, although he claimed that neither of them learned anything there. He remembered Dylan as not being a normal child, in the sense that he was able to recite entire speeches from Shakespeare plays, and that his molly-coddling mother Florrie would allow him to stay away from school for trivial reasons, supposedly to do with his ill-health. They were to enjoy a lifelong friendship.

When Levy moved to London, where he studied at the Royal College of Art, he stayed with Dylan and Fred Janes in Fulham. In 1935, as a student at the Royal College of Art, he received the Sir Herbert Read Prize for Drawing, and the American writer and painter Wyndham Lewis presented him with an envelope containing his prize of £2. He drew Dylan and, as they shared a similar sense of humour, the pair played, socialised and clowned around together. On one occasion they discussed how many mice it would take to haul a train to Glasgow from London. Sometimes they went together to Augustus John's place.

During the Second World War Levy attended the Royal Military College at Sandhurst, and became a captain in the Royal Army Educational Corps. When the war ended he went into the arts, lecturing overseas on the arts and touring Gibraltar and Germany. He then took a series of teaching posts in Bristol, where Dylan went to visit him when he was supposed to be attending an event for doctors in Swansea, and with London University. There's a story told that when Levy asked Dylan if he might bring along a sergeant who wanted to meet him, Dylan asked if Levy thought the sergeant would lend him £100. Levy said he would. Dylan left the meeting with a cheque, as expected.

In the 1950s Levy was given his own BBC TV series *Painting For Housewives* which made him a national figure. He became a regular guest on BBC radio arts broadcasts. During the next three decades he published twenty-five books, including *The Paintings of D.H. Lawrence*, and was an acknowledged expert on the Lancashire artist LS Lowry. He became features editor of *The Studio* magazine, interviewing the Spanish surrealist painter Dali in Spain. In the 1970s and 1980s he became fascinated with Art Nouveau. His portrait of Dylan was exhibited in the National Portrait Gallery in London. He was known as an intelligent, generous, witty and open-minded man who, like

Dylan, loved words and convivial company. He married three times and died in London in 1996.

## John Prichard

John Prichard was born in 1916 and became an award-winning novelist, short story writer and poet. Sadly, today he is not as well remembered as many of Dylan's other contemporaries and friends.

With Dylan, Fred Janes, Vernon Watkins and Dan Jones, Pritchard was one of the participants in the 1949 BBC programme *Swansea and the Arts* which was recorded in the Grove recording studios situated in Swansea's Uplands. In that programme, Dylan said of him, 'John Prichard, writer, I can best introduce, perhaps, by saying that he is the only conspirator among us. He conspires with the leagues of silence against his own remarkably articulate stories, with the dark gangs against his own peculiar, penetrating, lopsidedly smiling light. He lets his stories slip out, guiltily, like secrets.' He died in 1989.

## Bert Trick

Albert Edward Trick was a Swansea socialist and Labour Party member who lived not far from the Thomas' house. About twenty-five years older than Dylan, he had been an engineer until he lost his job in the economic depression, and later opened a grocery store in Brynmill. He was a big fan of books, politics, conversation and argument. He met Dylan in the early thirties, and both he and his wife Nell vigorously encouraged Dylan to read and publish his poems. In fact Trick claimed that it was he who persuaded a very reluctant Dylan to submit 'And death shall have no dominion' to the *New English Weekly*. Dylan told Trick that poems should be spoken rather than read, while Trick was particularly taken with what he described as Dylan's 'cathedral' voice, and urged him to develop the rich, dramatic style with which the world is now familiar.

Dylan saw the older man as a sort of political mentor, referring to him as a socialist grocer, and learned much about Socialism and Marxism from him. Dylan visited the Tricks' house regularly for social evenings, and the activities of Trick and his circle form the backdrop to Dylan's story 'Where Tawe Flows'. Trick noted Dylan's tendency to appear with a cigarette stuck in his lips as if for theatrical effect, as well as his use of vulgar language whenever he felt like it, but he enjoyed Dylan's acerbic wit and visited Cwmdonkin Drive for regular chats. The slow gestation of *Under Milk Wood* can be gauged by the fact that while Dylan was still a journalist in Swansea he told Trick that he had a plan for a story about the dreams of the inhabitants of a row of terraced houses in a place he was going to call Llaregub.

Trick wrote for the *Western Express* and the *West Wales Guardian*, so he and Dylan shared working experience in the newspaper trade. After Swansea was bombed, Dylan walked through the damaged town centre with Trick. Upset at what he saw, Dylan lamented, 'Our Swansea is dead'. In his notebook, Dylan's 1933 poem 'The hand that signed the paper' is dedicated 'To A.E.T'. Dylan often wrote to Trick, sometimes in detailed intellectual terms, and in one letter he expressed his antagonism towards the war, admitting that he could generate no feeling for it and refusing to help it with a bayonet. In another he told Trick of the birth of his son Llewelyn and described him as 'militantly Welsh'. Trick's also mentioned fondly in *Return Journey*, where it is said he 'threatened the annihilation of the ruling classes over sandwiches and jelly and blancmange.'

He died in 1968.

## Wynford Vaughan-Thomas

The noted broadcaster and journalist was born Wynford Lewis Vaughan-Thomas in Swansea in 1908. His father, Dr. David Vaughan Thomas, was a Professor of Music. His mother was Morfydd Lewis, the daughter of one of the leaders of the Rebecca riots in Pontardulais which were the subject of a film for which the screenplay was written by Dylan.

Vaughan-Thomas attended Swansea Grammar School where he was a pupil of Dylan's father DJ whom he remembered for, among other things, his violent temper, his love of literature and his fine voice. He departed Swansea for Oxford to study Modern History. In the mid 1930s he was taken on by the BBC, and in 1937 provided the Welsh commentary during the broadcast of the Coronation of King George VI, the first of many live broadcasts he was to deliver on important state occasions, and he was selected as a key member of the BBC's panel of commentators for the Coronation of Queen Elizabeth II. During the Second World War he became one of the BBC's most admired war correspondents. One report, well remembered to this day among radio aficionados, was from an RAF Lancaster during a bombing raid over Berlin. He also reported from Anzio in Italy, Lord Haw Haw's infamous broadcasting studio, and Belsen concentration camp in in northwestern Germany. He also commentated on the funeral of his wartime BBC colleague Richard Dimbleby who passed on in 1965.

Having left the BBC, in 1967 he became one of the founders, and Director of Programmes, of what is now ITV Wales. He was the author of several books, his topics including Wales and the Welsh countryside, and continued to broadcast on television. A well-known figure in his day, he was called on to officiate at numerous public events, including the opening of the Pembrokeshire coastal path where it starts in Amroth. Many observed that during his career with the broadcaster he projected a standard BBC accent, but after he left he reverted to his more natural Welsh accent.

Vaughan-Thomas had intermittent contact with Dylan over the years, both in Swansea and in London. They acted together at the Little Theatre in Swansea, and while Dylan was working as a reporter in the town he took Vaughan-Thomas with him on a journalistic assignment to interview the music hall performer Nellie Wallace. Vaughan-Thomas had just come back from Oxford, and taking their cue from rumours of a rabies epidemic, he and Dylan indulged in a spot of playful, if immature fun, pretending to be dogs and biting people's legs. Dylan wrote to Vaughan-Thomas, in one letter unashamedly, and astutely as it turned out, advising his friend to keep his letters, which he did.

In 1949 Vaughan-Thomas was the link-man for the BBC tv programme *Home Town – Swansea* which featured Dylan as well as Vernon Watkins, Fred Janes and Dan Jones. After Dylan's death he served as a trustee for the Dylan Thomas Trust, taking over from Dan Jones in 1955, although Dylan biographer George Tremlett felt he did not understand the full importance of the poet and his work to his (Tremlett's) generation.

He died in Fishguard in 1987. A memorial was erected in 1990 near Aberhosan looking towards the rolling slopes, with a depiction of the man himself pointing in the direction of Mount Snowdon.

**Vernon Watkins**

Vernon Watkins was born in Maesteg to his mother Sarah, who loved literature, and a father who was a committed Congregationalist with a great love of the Bible. Vernon was able to read by the time he was four, and at five declared his intention of becoming a poet. He also stipulated, somewhat precociously, that he only wanted to be published after he died. He composed poems long before he had reached double figures and read widely, especially of the works of Shelley and Keats. So with all that, and growing up around Swansea, his background and upbringing had many similarities with Dylan's.

Watkin's father William managed Lloyds Bank in Wind Street in Swansea, and the Watkins family lived at Redcliffe, Caswell Bay, a few miles from Swansea. Vernon was educated in Sussex, Derbyshire and Magdalene College, Cambridge. His headmaster in Derbyshire was Dr. Fisher, later Archbishop of Canterbury, and Watkins later joined the Church of England. He left Cambridge before completing his degree, and entered a troubled phase at the end of the 1920s, finding it difficult to handle the vicissitudes that life visited upon him. He took on a position with a bank in Cardiff before experiencing a complete nervous collapse, and spent time in a mental hospital in Derbyshire. While there he attempted to jump from a window in the belief that angels would catch him. He returned to work, at Lloyds bank in Cardiff in 1925, before transferring to their St Helen's Road branch in Swansea. He was to stay there for most of his life, his main concern being to ensure he had enough time to apply to his poetry.

He and Dylan had met in 1935 in Swansea. Nearly every week Dylan would visit the Watkins home perched on the cliffs of the Gower peninsula. He was one of the few people Dylan heeded when seeking a response to his poems, and such was Dylan's trust in his friend's literary judgement that he was often the first person to see Dylan's latest work. Dylan often made good-natured fun out of

Watkin's delicate personality and sensitivity, once claiming that his friend and confidante had fallen over a feather on the pavement. Dylan agreed to perform the role of best man at his friend's wedding to his wife Gwen, but let them down by not turning up on the day. Yet they stayed friends until Dylan's death, and Watkins served as godfather to Dylan's older son Llewelyn. He wrote a warm obituary for Dylan, and when he himself died, Philip Larkin wrote his.

It is arguable that Watkins, apart from the poet's parents or Caitlin, knew Dylan as both man and poet better than anyone else. He described the early stories of Dylan's as very Welsh and 'more true to Swansea than Swansea itself'. Watkins is believed to have found the last, alas unfinished, poem by Dylan, a work that related to DJ's fathers' death. He published the book *Letters to Vernon Watkins* in 1957, containing letters Dylan had sent him over the years. In 1983 the book *Portrait of a Friend*, written by Gwen Watkins, covered the friendship between the two poets.

# Dylan in Music

There's been some speculation, and not without considerable supporting evidence, that, had he lived, the next phase of Dylan's career would have seen him moving into writing libretti for operas. As a lifelong music fan who has spend virtually all my career in the music industry and the music media, and who discovered Dylan through a musical connection, this is news I'd certainly have welcomed with open arms and open ears.

There was serious talk of him starting a collaboration with the Russian composer Igor Stravinsky after what was to become his last American tour. An earlier project involving both of them had fallen through when the expected funding failed to materialise.

Stravinsky, born in Leningrad in 1882, spent some time in France before moving to the USA during the Second World War and became a naturalised American citizen. During Dylan's visit to the US in the first half of 1953 he met with Stravinsky at the Copley Plaza Hotel in Boston to discuss possible subjects for a Stravinsky opera. Afterwards, Dylan told Caitlin that he and she would soon be heading for Hollywood. He outlined his expectations of a £500 advance, plus travel costs, and then 'royalties until we die'.

Dylan was very energised by his meeting with Stravinsky, and wrote to the composer telling him he planned to go to California to meet him after his next (tragically ill-fated) American tour. I've no doubt that Dylan was keen to pursue the idea of this collaboration with one of the towering figures of the classical world, already of major international renown through such works as *The Rite of Spring* and *The Fire Bird.* Dylan even discussed a possible scenario for the intended opera with his biographer Constantine Fitzgibbon.

It was wrongly hoped that sponsorship could be found that would enable Dylan and Caitlin to live in the USA during this creative process. Indeed, so serious was the composer about the plan that he had his house adapted to create living accommodation for Dylan. Of course, I suspect that the prospect of Dylan living in Hollywood might well have had its own problems. There had been brief talk of a fee of $12,000, but more than likely Dylan would've had to pay his living expenses from more poetry recitals, so money would have been, as ever, a difficulty, and Caitlin was understandably anxious about the possibility of Dylan being away from her watchful and wary eye.

I see Dylan's involvement in such a venture as a natural extension of his portfolio of creative activities that had already included articles, poems, short stories, film scripts, radio talks, poetry recitals, a novel and a play for voices. The writing of operas might well have been where his creative urge would take him next. Stravinsky had already collaborated with the English author WH Auden on *The Rake's Progress* and it was Auden who had suggested to Stravinsky that he should link up with Dylan. Sadly, Dylan's death put an end to the idea, although in 1954, the two had a posthumous collaboration of sorts when Stravinsky composed *In Memoriam* in honour of the poet, using Dylan's 'Do not go gentle into that good night' as the text of a work for tenor voice, string quartet, and four trombones.

Nor would the planned musical venture have been out of place in Dylan's oeuvre. He had included some songs in *Under Milk Wood*, and apart from the obvious musicality of his verse, he had been interested in music composition from a very young age. A musical version of *Under Milk Wood* (with songs by George Martin and Elton John) was conceived by the Llandeilo author Lynn Hughes who had spotted Dylan's notes on his script suggesting 'more songs & music'. But back as early as 1928, Dylan had collaborated with his friend Daniel Jones on writing songs and operatic pieces, Jones playing piano and composing the music, with Dylan taking care of the lyrics. Their earliest work was probably 'Vier Lieder' (Four Songs). They also amused themselves by inventing names for the supposed composer of such pieces, including that of Max Tonenbach.

Over the years I've made a note of the connections between Dylan and music. The list gets longer every year, and even what follows might not be comprehensive.

**1959** Peter Dickinson composed his *Dylan Thomas Song Cycle* in New York, setting some of Dylan's most famous poems. That same year, a man from Minnesota born Robert Zimmerman made his first public performance as a folk singer using the name Bob Dylan. It was rumoured that the new name was borrowed from Dylan Thomas, but the singer has refuted this. However, there is no doubt that he was familiar with the Welsh man's work, and in his 2004 biography, *Chronicles Vol.1*, he clarified matters somewhat by saying that Dylan Thomas influenced his name-change, but only because he preferred the spelling 'Dylan' to the alternative 'Dillon'. Bob Dylan's 1963 song 'When the Ship Comes In' features the phrase, 'the chains of the sea', and it takes little effort to see the link with the final line 'I sang in my chains like the sea' from Thomas's 'Fern Hill' poem. Furthermore, Dylan's girlfriend Suze Rotolo, pictured with Dylan on the cover of his second album, wondered about his 'Welsh' name, so she too was clearly familiar with the Welsh origins of his adopted name.

**1965** The English jazz pianist Stan Tracey released his interpretation of *Under Milk Wood*. It has since become one of the most acclaimed British jazz albums of all time.

**1966** The song, 'A Simple Desultory Philippic (Or How I Was Robert McNamara'd Into Submission)', recorded by Simon and Garfunkel and written by Paul Simon, included the humorous line, 'He's so unhip, that when you say Dylan, he thinks you're talking about Dylan Thomas, Whoever he was.' So even by the mid-sixties, Thomas' reputation had already infiltrated the American folk and pop music scene.

**1967** The cover of the Beatles album *Sgt. Pepper's Lonely Hearts Club Band* included a photograph of Dylan Thomas as part the front montage created by the artist Peter Blake and Jann Haworth. It's believed that Dylan's inclusion was suggested by John Lennon.

**1972** Using the pseudonym 'Robert Milkwood Thomas', Bob Dylan sang and played on the title track of the album *Somebody Else's Troubles* by American singer-songwriter Steve Goodman. The adopted name is an obvious conflation of Dylan Thomas and *Under Milk Wood*.

**1974** The British progressive rock band King Crimson released an album called *Starless and Bible Black*, the phrase a quotation from the poet Dylan's *Under Milk Wood*.

**1988** A Musical version of *Under Milk Wood* (with songs by George Martin and Elton John) was issued as a double-album. The project also involved Sir Anthony Hopkins, Tom Jones and Bonnie Tyler.

**1989** Ammanford-born Welsh rock singer and songwriter John Cale released his album *Words for the Dying*. It contained his thirty-one-minute long 'Falklands Suite' in which he recorded settings of four Dylan Thomas poems ('There was a saviour', 'Do not go gentle into that good night', 'On a Wedding Anniversary', and 'Lie still, sleep becalmed') with a Russian orchestra and a Welsh choir. Also in 1989, composer Gary Backlund's *Voices Under Milk Wood* set sections of the play for medium high voice and piano.

**1990** The song 'Dog's Eyes, Owl Meat and Man Chop' released on *The Domino Club* album by The Men They Couldn't Hang, relates to Dylan Thomas and Wales. The title is directly taken from a line uttered by the character Butcher Beynon in *Under Milk Wood*. Welsh rock singer John Cale's solo live album *Fragments of a Rainy Season* contained live versions of settings of three Thomas poems which he had previously released in studio versions.

**1994** The Rev Eli Jenkins' Prayer from *Under Milk Wood* was set to the music of an Anglican chant by AHD Troyte. The Dunvant Male Voice Choir were filmed singing it by Rhossili Bay. The Pennsylvanian rock band The Gathering Field included a song called 'Dylan Thomas Days' on their self-titled debut album.

**1995** The composer Henri Lazarof from Sofia in Bulgaria published his *Encounters with Dylan Thomas*, a choral piece for soprano and chamber ensemble.

**1999** John Corigliano composed *A Dylan Thomas Trilogy* as a memory play in the form of an oratorio.

**2000** Robin Williamson's CD *The Seed-At-Zero* contained the songs 'The Seed-At-Zero', 'Holy Spring', 'In My Craft or Sullen Art', 'On No Work of Words', 'Hold Hard, These Ancient Minutes in The Cuckoo's Month' and 'Poem On His Birthday', all with words by Dylan Thomas and music by Williamson. It also includes Williamson's song 'For Mr Thomas'.

**2002** In his song 'There She Goes, My Beautiful World', the Australian rock singer Nick Cave sings the line 'Dylan Thomas, he died drunk in St. Vincent's Hospital'.

**2004** The Scottish-born folksinger Donovan, once touted as the new Bob Dylan and now living in Ireland, released his album *Beat Cafe*. It contained the track 'Do Not Go Gentle', described as a poem by Dylan Thomas, music by Donovan Leitch.

**2004** Ralph McTell released an album called *The Boy With A Note*, described as an evocation of the life of Dylan Thomas in words and music. As part of the concert held in Cardiff to celebrate the opening of the Welsh Assembly, John Cale performed his setting of 'Do not go gentle into that good night'.

**2006** The rock band The Slip included a reference to Thomas in their song, 'Airplane/Primitive' which contained the line 'It is the day before the rest of my life, and I feel like Dylan Thomas'.

**2010** *Canu'r Wenallt* (Songs from Milk Wood), an original piece of music inspired by *Under Milk Wood*, was performed for the first time. The female choir Côr Merched Canna commissioned the work from composer Gareth Glyn. That same year, Swansea-based jazz musician Jen Wilson recorded *Twelve Poems: The Dylan Thomas Jazz Suite*, an album of songs inspired by Dylan. The Welsh tenor Bryn Terfel has issued an album *We'll Keep A Welcome* which included 'Sunset Poem, Eli Jenkin's Prayer'.

**2012** A track called 'Gweddi Eli Jenkins' appeared on the album *Llanw A Thrai* by Ar Ol Tri on the Fflach label. It's a Welsh language version of the Rev Eli Jenkins' Prayer from *Under Milk Wood*.

# Dylan's Irish Connections

The project *A Map of Love: Around Wales With Dylan Thomas* is a joint Welsh-Irish venture under the CORACLE scheme that links West Wales with South-East Ireland. The scheme provided a welcome opportunity to tease out my own reactions to Dylan's work, and the places associated with him, from my own Irish perspective. It's also given me the chance to explore Dylan Thomas' Irish connections, especially as his wife Caitlin was Irish.

As Celtic nations the Irish and the Welsh have much in common, and some parts of Wales are physically closer to Ireland than to the bigger English cities of Birmingham and London. But Irish people have been slow to discover Wales, and I am not the only person to have publicly wondered why so little effort was made to attract Irish tourists to holiday in Wales, although I'm very pleased that this has been addressed with a concerted campaign in 2011.

Of course many Irish people would have travelled

through Wales en route to the bigger English cities, Liverpool and Birmingham, but the pressure of heading on to one's destination, coupled with a lack of effort to encourage them to stop, has meant that Irish people in general are not as aware of the delights of the Welsh landscape as they might be. I've done a little to spread the word, having reported back to base about very pleasant holidays in Betws-y-coed, Snowdonia, Conwy and Harlech, as well as those places connected with Dylan and mentioned in the main text. But in the course of my readings about Dylan I noticed many connections to Ireland.

The first mass-market biography of the poet, *The Life of Dylan Thomas*, was published in 1965 and written by Constantine Fitzgibbon who, although born in Massachusetts, moved to Ireland in 1965, became an Irish citizen and died in Dublin in 1983. He had been friends with Dylan and his wife-to-be during the war, as had the woman he married Theodora Fitzgibbon. The marriage failed. I knew Theodora, who was a writer and cookery correspondent with the *Irish Times*, one of our leading national daily newspapers. She was a formidable woman, not averse to using her power and prominence to make public relations personnel dance attendance on her. I met Constantine at a press reception once and we spoke about the dissident Russian writer Aleksandr Solzhenitsyn who was a topic of international conversation at the time on account of the filming of his book *One Day in the Life of Ivan Denisovich*. All I can now recall of that conversation was the way he pronounced the writer's name in the Russian way, and not as we in Ireland pronounced it. It struck me as an irritating affectation back then, but now I admire him for it.

Another friendship that grew from Dylan's London days was that with the poet Louis MacNeice who was born in Belfast in 1907. In 1938 they were both contributors to a poetry reading in Manchester for the BBC under the title *The Modern Muse*. In 1946 Dylan played the part of Aristophanes in a BBC radio comedy drama *Enemies of Cant*, written by MacNeice, who also cast Dylan in the part of a raven in the fairytale drama *The Heartless Giant*. There is a recording of Dylan reading 'The Libertine' by MacNeice.

At one point there was a plan for Dylan to travel with MacNeice to Belfast where it was intended that Dylan would recite 'The Hare' by WR Rodgers. Unfortunately, the trip was aborted at the last minute because Dylan, allegedly, was reported to be suffering from food poisoning. 'Lent', a poem by Rodgers, was one of the many poems by Irish poets that found a place in Dylan's recital repertoire.

His friendship with MacNeice was such that Dylan was invited to stay with him in Canonbury in London, and they drank regularly in such London watering dens as The Dover Castle and The George And Stag. They once attempted to attend a cricket match at Lords, only to arrive after the game had ended. They then went on to a different match at The Oval, before ending the day by attending a show at the London Casino. The Irishman, who worked at the BBC, said that Dylan took his radio acting very seriously, and was a joy to have around the studio, despite causing some anxiety to the studio managers with his unpredictable behaviour.

MacNeice wrote about Dylan's funeral in his 1954 poem *Autumn Sequel*. He described going to Wales 'once more, though not on holiday'. He refers to Dylan as Gwilym and mentions black shoes he bought with Dylan in London's Regent Street to wear to the funeral of Yeats. The Belfastman's poem includes references to Swansea, Sir John's Hill and November 25th, the day after Dylan's burial. He was later active in trying to raise funds to help support Caitlin and the children, and read from his personal tribute to Dylan at a fundraising event at the Globe Theatre in London.

While the aforementioned planned trip to Belfast had been aborted, Dylan did make a couple of journeys across the Irish Sea for holidays, and at a time when travel, even across the comparatively short watery gap, was not as easy or as comfortable as it is now. He was also aware of some of that country's great writers, especially WB Yeats and James Joyce.

In 1946 the editor of *Horizon* magazine Cyril Connolly asked him what he thought was the best second occupation for a poet. Giving Yeats as an example of a poet who had become financially secure through attracting patronage so that he could write and think about nothing but poetry, Dylan reckoned a poet still needed to give himself another job, that of 'philosopher, mystic, crank, quack'. Academics have observed that Dylan's poem 'In Borrowed Plumes' copies Yeats' style, and he refers dismissively, although perhaps playfully, to 'Yeats' voice' among a long list of subjects which he feels are of no more importance than a squirrel stumbling. A recording I have of Yeats reciting his famous poem 'The Lake Isle of Inisfree' offers a complete contrast in reading styles. Whereas Dylan's delivery is full-bodied and dramatic, Yeats' is at times melodramatic and, to my ears, old-fashioned.

As for Joyce, some commentators see clear echoes in aspects of *Under Milk Wood* of the Circe section of the Irish author's novel *Ulysses*. Dylan refers to 'James Joyce's mental slummings' in his *A Letter To My Aunt Discussing the Correct Approach to Poetry*. The title for Dylan's story collection *Portrait Of the Artist As A Young Dog* seems likely to have been borrowed from Joyce's *A Portrait of the Artist As A Young Man* which was also largely autobiographical. But although he admitted to much admiration for Joyce and to have enjoyed both *Ulysses* and Joyce's stories, he denied that the Irish writer had a influence on his published poetry, and even suggested that the title *Portrait Of the Artist As A Young Dog* could just have easily been inspired by the many paintings of a similar title. Just as much of Dylan's work comes alive when recited aloud, the Irish senator and former Presidential candidate David Norris once advised me that the best way to read Joyce's complex *Finnegans Wake* (sic) was to do so aloud so as to appreciate the melodiousness of the work.

Among the broad repertoire of works he selected for

public readings and radio broadcasts were poems by Yeats, including 'In Tara's Halls', 'The Three Bushes' and 'Lapis Lazuli', as well as works by the Irish writer and nationalist Donagh MacDonagh, and Oliver St John Gogarty, a friend of James Joyce who features as Buck Mulligan in *Ulysses*. His radio recordings included a reading of the poem 'A Glass of Beer' by the Dublin poet and novelist James Stephens. Around the time of his relationship with Pamela Hansford Johnson, Dylan attended a play by controversial playwright Sean O'Casey in London, and he read from that man's writings too. So as an avid reader and student of great literature, Dylan was not only familiar with the Irish greats of international renown such as MacNeice, Yeats and Joyce, but also with also with lesser-known figures such as Liam O'Flaherty. Time, and other less convincing excuses, have been used by Irish people, including myself, for not being as familiar with the works of our own authors as we should, and Dylan's interest certainly acts as a spur to rectifying that situation.

But he was no uncritical reader. When he reviewed Samuel Beckett's novel *Murphy* he dismissed the Irish Nobel Laureate's 'Freudian blarney'. But he was more favourably disposed to the County Tyrone-born Flann O'Brien's novel *At- Swim-Two-Birds*, seeing it as part of the vanguard of modern Irish literature. Dylan's broad-ranging familiarity with things Irish can be seen in his reference to 'a tree on Aran' in the poem 'I, in my intricate image', Aran being an island off the west coast of Ireland.

Of course, the most crucial Irish connection in Dylan's life was his wife Caitlin Macnamara, whose parents were landowners in Ireland. Caitlin, whom Dylan referred to punningly as his 'cattleanchor', was born in Hammersmith, London, in 1913 to the self-styled Irish poet Francis Macnamara and his French-Irish wife Yvonne. Caitlin had three older siblings, a brother John and two sisters, Nicolette and Brigid.

Francis was given the nickname Fireball, and his father owned estates worth £10,000 at Ennistymon House, a Georgian mansion not far from Ennistymon in County Clare in the west of Ireland. When Caitlin visited the area she described herself as being intoxicated by the surrounding countryside, including its stone walls and roads. Ennistymon is only two miles from the Atlantic Ocean, one more connection between Dylan and the sea.

Francis mixed with artists and writers, including Augustus John who painted in the County Clare area. The painter, who was later to figure in Dylan's life at various times, stayed with the family, and is believed to have had a relationship with Yvonne. While Caitlin was still a child, Francis left the family home in an unsuccessful attempt to establish himself as a writer. So, Yvonne took command of the family and they moved to the New Forest where Augustus John was a close neighbour. There were even unsubstantiated rumours that he was actually her father.

Caitlin grew into a vivacious and outspoken, sometimes aggressively offensive young woman, reputed to have attracted a parade of male admirers. She was later to become the subject of intense rivalry between John and Dylan, resulting on one occasion in a violent altercation.

In 1930, still in her mid-teens, she moved to London to take up dancing, but with little success. She accompanied her father when he went back to his family's properties in County Clare in 1934 and stayed there for some time. The family mansion had by this time been converted into the Falls Hotel, and Caitlin worked in the bar, painted and wrote. She also lived in Paris with a painter for a year.

In 1936 she came back to London where she is believed to have met Dylan Thomas in either the Wheatsheaf pub or the Fitzroy, depending on whose account you believe. It was not long until they began what turned out to be an often turbulent relationship that lasted until Dylan's death, with both partners suspected of infidelity on several occasions over the years.

In 1937 they were married in Penzance in Cornwall, but they lived in numerous places throughout a married life that, through the demands of Dylan's career, often saw them spending long periods apart. Caitlin had kept contact with Ireland through her many visits there, and believed that Dylan wanted her to be a lovely, lovelorn, Irish peasant lass. She was convinced that he had an intellectual side that he hid from her with his 'Welsh shrewd sense'. In her autobiography *Double Drink Story*, she admits that neither her not Dylan had the slightest idea as to what the other was like inside, and that each was willing to put up with the other's ego so as it didn't interfere with their own.

Dylan was attracted by Caitlin's carefree nature, although his mother was not impressed by her gypsy-style dresses. She thought nothing of bathing naked, and she indulged in such unladylike tasks as rolling her own cigarettes at a time when such unconventional activities were frowned on. Yet in spite of their freewheeling outward lifestyle, Caitlin maintained that they were both 'puritanically inclined' in private. Given her own background, her father's interest in the literature and the arts, as well as her own artistic inclinations, she must have been drawn, at least partly, to Dylan for his literary talent. Their relationship influenced his work too. His poem 'On A Wedding Anniversary' is almost certainly written to mark their third wedding anniversary. Another work, 'Poem (to Caitlin)', is by no means celebratory, and suggests a man not at ease with himself. After showing it to Vernon Watkins he made vast changes to it.

Of course, Caitlin made many personal sacrifices and suffered much hardship in order to enable Dylan to follow his muse. However, her commitment to Dylan undoubtedly thwarted her own writing and dancing ambitions, and despite her sometimes dismissive attitude towards him and his work, she was very protective of him.

The night before his last and ill-fated trip to the USA, Caitlin and Dylan went to the cinema in Carmarthen and then journeyed from Laugharne through Swansea to London. They stayed with friends in Hammersmith and did some shopping, drinking, dining and took in a visit to the theatre, while Dylan also had a drink with Constantine Fitzgibbon in London. Caitlin made it obvious to their friends that she was opposed to Dylan's pending New York trip.

After his death in November 1953, she moved to Italy, where she remarried and had another son, Francesco, at the age of forty-nine. Caitlin was the author and/or subject of several books that focus on her life with Dylan, including one with George Tremlett, called *Caitlin – A Warring Absence*, and the autobiographical *My Life With Dylan Thomas – Double Drink Story*, in which she graphically described their life together. In the latter she wrote 'Dylan killed himself with false heroics, trying to make the poet more important than his poetry, selling the poet instead of selling the poetry'. She died in Sicily in 1994.

## Dylan in Ireland

Dylan's visits to Ireland were basically for holidays rather than having any serious literary intent. In 1935 he went to Donegal in the north-west of Ireland, accompanied by the noted poet and critic Geoffrey Grigson, of whom he was a little wary. The two are reported to have stayed in a donkey shed converted into a studio in Adara, and to have eaten healthy local food such as buttermilk and potatoes. Dylan grew a beard, and they enjoyed long strolls by the nearby Atlantic Ocean and are reported to have shouted 'we are the dead' at the hills late at night. I could not help noticing that their chosen location was yet another example of Dylan spending time near the sea.

Dylan took the time to write a long, openly emotional and nostalgic letter to his long-term friend Daniel Jones during this holiday. He also revised his poem 'Grief thief of time', and is also believed to have worked on 'Altarwise by owl-light'. But the Donegal idyll was not to last, as after two weeks Grigson discovered he had to return to London, leaving Dylan alone, albeit with sufficient money for rent and other essentials. Dylan decided to spend the money on other things that were far more important to him, and went back to London penniless. Dylan had written to Bert Trick, after Grigson's departure, complaining of loneliness. Grigson claimed that his happiest memories of Dylan were from that Donegal trip.

In 1946, Dylan and Caitlin took a late summer holiday in Kerry with Bill McAlpine and his wife Helen, the latter of whom Caitlin was particularly fond. They could, without much inconvenience, have detoured to Ennistymon, but appear not to have done so, some say because Caitlin was ashamed of the place.

Dylan was attracted to this part of Ireland through having worked on the film script adaptation of the book *Twenty Years A-Growing* by Maurice O'Sullivan during his stay at Majoda in New Quay. The original work is based on O'Sullivan's memories of growing up in the early part of the twentieth century on the remote Blasket Islands situated off the coast of Kerry. In a life that has echoes of Dylan's early adventures around Swansea and Fern Hill, O'Sullivan spent his youth communing with nature, exploring crevices in the cliffs, fishing in the sea and chasing rabbits.

Bill McAlpine hailed from Ulster and was an ardent admirer of James Joyce. En route to the south-west of Ireland, the quartet had four days in Dublin, the home of Joyce and James Stephens, whom Dylan also greatly admired, as well as the playwright and garrulous raconteur Brendan Behan. I've already noted some of the parallels between Dylan and Behan and their respective lifestyles. They both scandalised society with their outspoken comments and outrageous behaviour, especially when fuelled by drink or the need for attention (or both). They both applied an acerbic deprecatory wit to all and sundry, and both died early, Behan aged forty-one, Dylan even younger at thirty-nine. It may have been a good thing that, as far as we know, they never met. But then again...

The vacationing quartet's destination in County Kerry was the town of Killorglin, the site of the annual Puck Fair, about which Dylan had been commissioned to write an article for *Picture Post* and for which he had been paid an advance. While there, Dylan took a day trip out to the Blasket Islands to see the specific area in which O'Sullivan had grown up. As he wrote to his great benefactor Margaret Taylor back in England 'The wind blew me about like a tissue-paper man'. He also told her, 'We had breathless days in Ireland', and expressed his delight in the food and drink they had enjoyed in Dublin. As Dylan told Vernon Watkins on his return from Ireland, 'We ate ourselves daft.'

So, with far more important matters on his mind, the article for *Picture Post* doesn't seem to have ever materialised.

When Caitlin wrote about the Puck Fair adventure in her memoir *My Life With Dylan Thomas – Double Drink Story* she claimed that while in Kerry, Dylan and Bill drank Guinness for two days and two nights non-stop, forty-eight consecutive hours. According to her, they were both still standing in the same spot in which they had started. This has struck me as probably physically and medically impossible, and apart from foolishly reinforcing the exaggerated reputation Dylan has gained for his drinking capacity, it also casts doubt on the veracity of some other aspects of her tales. Sadly, we may never know the truth.

# Dylan
# Essentials

# Key Works

Poetry collections:
*18 Poems* (1934)
*New Poems* (1934 USA)
*Twenty-Five Poems* (1936)
*Deaths and Entrances* (1946)
*In Country Sleep and Other Poems* (1952 USA)
*Collected Poems 1934-1953* (1998)
*The Notebook Poems 1930-1934* (1989)

Poetry and Prose collections:
*The Map of Love* (1939)
*The World I Breathe* (1939)
*Selected Writings of Dylan Thomas* (1946 USA)

Play:
*Under Milk Wood* (available in book, film, musical and cartoon versions)

Prose Works:
*Adventures In the Skin Trade* (1955)
*The Death of The King's Canary*, with John Davenport (1978)
*Portrait of the Artist As A Young Dog* (1940)
*Collected Stories* (1983)
*Selected Letters* – edited by Constantine Fitzgibbon (1966)
*The Collected Letters* – edited by Paul Ferris (1985)

Biographies and Critical Works – a selection:

*Leftover Life To Kill* by Caitlin Thomas (1957)

*Dylan Thomas; the Legend and the Poet*, edited by EW Tedlock (1960)

*Dylan Thomas* by TH Jones (1963)

*The Days of Dylan Thomas – A Pictorial Biography* by Rollie McKenna (1964)

*Dylan Thomas – A Collection of Critical Essays* edited by CB Cox (1966)

*The Growth of Milk Wood* by Douglas Cleverdon (1969)

*Dylan Thomas – Poet of His People* by Andrew Sinclair (1975)

*Dylan Thomas The Biography* by Paul Ferris (1977)

*Welsh Dylan* by John Ackerman (1979)

*Dylan Thomas – In The Mercy of His Mea*ns by George Tremlett (1991)

*My Life With Dylan Thomas – Double Drink Stor*y by Caitlin Thomas (1998)

*Dylan Thomas – A New Life* by Andrew Lycett (2003)

*My Father's Places* by Aeronwy Thomas (2009)

# Milestones

**27 October 1914**

Dylan Marlais Thomas was born to DJ and Florence
Thomas at 5 Cwmdonkin Drive.

**1925**

He enrolled at Swansea Grammar School. His father
taught English there.

**December 1925**

Dylan's first poem was published in the school magazine.

**1929**

Dylan's essay *Modern Poetry* was published in the school
magazine.

**April 1930**

He started the first of four notebooks containing his
poetry.

**1931**

Dylan became a reporter with the *South Wales Evening
Post*.

**1932**

He quit his job at the *South Wales Evening Post*, although
he still worked for them for a while in a freelance capacity.

**1933**

His poem 'And Death Shall Have No Dominion' was
published in the *New English Weekly*.

He made his first visit to London.

**May 1934**

Dylan first visited Laugharne.

**November 1934**

His new collection *18 Poems* was published.

**1936**

Dylan met Caitlin Macnamara, his future wife.

*Twenty-five Poems* was published.

**April 1937**

Dylan made his first radio broadcast of many. It was called *Life and the Modern Poet.*

He and Caitlin married.

**March 1938**

Dylan began negotiations for the publication of his work in America.

**May 1938**

He and Caitlin moved to Laugharne.

**1939**

Dylan and Caitlin's first son Llewelyn was born.

*The Map of Love*, a collection of Dylan's poems and prose, was published.

**1940**

*Portrait of the Artist As A Young Dog*, a collection of Dylan's autobiographical stories, was published.

Dylan started to write film scripts.

**1943**

Their only daughter Aeronwy was born.

Dylan and his family moved to live with his parents at Llangain, close to Fern Hill.

**1944**

They moved to New Quay in Cardiganshire.

Dylan recorded *Quite Early One Morning* for the BBC.

**1945**

He recorded *Memories of Christmas* for the BBC.

**1946**

Dylan's poetry collection *Deaths and Entrances* was published.

**1948**

He stayed in Llangain with his father while his mother Florence was hospitalised.

**1949**

Dylan and his family moved into the Boathouse in Laugharne.

Their second son Colm was born in Carmarthen.

**1950**

Dylan undertook his first American tour.

**1952**

Dylan's goes on his second American tour, accompanied by Caitlin.

*Collected Poems 1934-1952* was published.

Dylan's father died.

**1953**

Dylan went on his third and fourth American tours.

He delivered the script of *Under Milk Wood* to the BBC.

**9 November 1953**

Dylan Thomas passed away in St Vincent's Hospital, New York. He was buried in Laugharne.

# Visiting Dylan's World

**Dylan's Birthplace**

Thanks to the generous co-operation of Anne and Geoff Haden, the enclosed CD was recorded in the very room where Dylan Thomas was born at 5 Cwmdonkin Drive, Swansea, imbuing the recording with a special resonance that would have been otherwise unattainable. Anne and Geoff both grew up in the Swansea suburbs around The Uplands, and played as children in Cwmdonkin Park, so they're acutely aware of the role the house and the surrounding area played in Dylan's development as a poet and as a man.

They're always happy to share and celebrate Dylan's birthplace which has been carefully restored to the condition it was in 1914 when it was purchased as a new house by Dylan's parents. Whenever they're asked why they restored a dwelling that was by then in some need of repair, they simply answer 'because we're mad about Dylan's writings.'

Indeed, this house is rather unique in the literary world, as it's now possible to stay there for a self-catering holiday or even just for one night. It can also be booked for a private house tour. As the Hadens astutely observe, 'Number 5 is not a museum, but a living house without cordoned off areas.' Dylan fans everywhere owe them a debt of gratitude for their work in preserving the poet's birthplace so lovingly.

For further details visit www.5cwmdonkindrive.com
telephone: +44(0)1792 405331
or e-mail info@5cwmdonkindrive.com

## The Dylan Thomas Centre, Swansea

The Dylan Thomas Centre is a focal point for studies and events based around Dylan Thomas.

The Dylan Thomas Centre has a permanent exhibition on Dylan Thomas and his life, as well as a shop replete with books, posters and memorabilia. It's located in a beautiful building in the Maritime Quarter of Swansea, and has an excellent restaurant. The Centre is also home to the Ty Llen literature programme which puts on many literary events throughout the year, including the annual Dylan Thomas Festival during October and November. Entry is free to the Centre's permanent exhibition, 'Dylan Thomas: Man and Myth'.

Opening hours are 10am – 4.30pm, seven days a week.

Dylan Thomas Centre, Somerset Place,
Swansea
SA1 1RR
Tel: 01792 463980
Fax: 01792 463993
E-mail: dylanthomas.lit@swansea.gov.uk

## The Boathouse, Laugharne

The Boathouse is arguably the main focus for Thomas fans as it was his last residence, and a major source of pleasure and inspiration to him. It's also in the town where he's buried. But apart from the close connection with the poet it's a delightful spot to visit, with its breathtaking views out over the estuary to the sea, its old castle and easy-going charm.

The house is now the property of Carmarthenshire County Council and has been lovingly preserved and turned into a fitting museum containing memorabilia associated with Dylan's life and an audio-visual display. It even retains some of the original fittings. Behind the house is the Dylan's famous writing shed.

The house attracts about 15,000 visitors every year, but unfortunately the house itself currently lacks wheelchair access, although the shed can be viewed and 'peeped into' from the pathway that runs above the house. The venue needs advance notice of large party visits, and there is a pleasant tea room on site that serves refreshments and home baking.

The Boathouse in Laugharne is open from May to October, as well as the Easter weekend:

From 10am - 5.30pm (last admission at 5pm)

From November to April

10.30am - 3.30pm (last admission at 3pm)

Admission charges at time of this publication:

Adult - £4

Concessions - £3

Family - £9

Children over 7 - £1.95

Children under 7 - FREE

Write to:

Dylan Thomas Boathouse

Dylan's Walk

Laugharne

SA33 4SD

Telephone: 01994 427420

Fax: 01994 427420

E-mail: boathouse@carmarthenshire.gov.uk

# Important Websites

www.dylanthomas.com

www.dylanthomasboathouse.com

www.fflach.co.uk

www.wexfordartscentre.ie

www.5cwmdonkindrive.com

www.thisisdylanthomas.co.uk

www.swansea.gov.uk/dtc

Coracle.eu.com

# ACKNOWLEDGEMENTS

Jackie Hayden would like to thank the following for their generous involvement, support and advice in relation to this project:

Jim Parc Nest (T James Jones)
Lucy Llewellyn (editor)
Lucy Caldwell (winner of Dylan Thomas Prize 2011)
Phil Alder (Carmarthenshire County Council and Coracle Project)
Jo Furber (Dylan Thomas Centre, Swansea)
Anne and Geoff Haden at 5 Cwmdonkin Drive, Swansea
Jon Turner
Frank Jenkins
Myles Pepper (West Wales Art Centre, Fishguard)
Jon Tregenna (author of the play Buggerall)
Elizabeth Whyte (Wexford Arts Centre and Coracle Project)
Richard and Wyn Jones (Fflach Records)
Dominic Williams (Iconau Books)
Dave Daly (cover photograph)
Caradog Rhys Williams
Tanya Murphy

# Fflach Records

The CD that comes with this book was produced by Fflach Records in Cardigan. Fflach Records is one of Wales' longest-established and most respected recording companies. It was set up in 1981 by the brothers Richard and Wyn Jones, both noted local musicians with a deep interest in a wide range of music. Apart from Welsh folk and choral music, and recordings in both Welsh and English, the Fflach group of labels also has an extensive catalogue of spoken art, pop and rock music by some of Wales' finest artists. Their records have been reviewed throughout Britain and Ireland, featured on radio stations all over the world and downloaded by fans as far away as Patagonia and Japan. Fflach also have a special section for children's CDs, and operate their own recording studios, publishing company and advisory service for young musicians.

For further details see www.fflach.co.uk

# Jim Parc Nest

Jim Parc Nest, who reads the CD that accompanies this book, is the bardic name of T James Jones, the highly-respected Welsh poet and dramatist. The brother of the Welsh-language writers John Gwilym Jones and Aled Gwyn, he grew up in Newcastle Emlyn and attended Aberystwyth University and Presbyterian College in Carmarthen. He became a Congregational minister in Mynydd Bach, Swansea and Priordy, Carmarthen, and has lectured in Welsh and Drama at Trinity College, Carmarthen. He has also worked as a script editor for the television station S4C's Welsh language drama series *Pobol y Cwm*. As a playwright he has written eight plays, including a Welsh translation of Dylan Thomas' 'play for voices' *Under Milk Wood*. In 2008 he recorded the CD *Cerddi Jim Parc Nest* which includes his 'Y pelican', a translation into Welsh of Dylan Thomas' poem 'Do Not Go Gentle Into That Good Night'.

In 2009 he was nominated as Archdruid of the National Eisteddfod, having won the crown twice previously and the chair once. Jim is married to the author Manon Rhys, and his uncle is the poet Tudur Dylan Jones.

# CD CREDITS

READER: T. James Jones
MUSIC & ARRANGEMENTS: Caradog Rhys Williams
© Mwldan Publications
TEXT: Jackie Hayden ©
PRODUCER:   Wyn Jones
RECORDED AT: 5 Cwmdonkin Drive, Swansea
EDITING and MASTERING: Jon Turner

1   Bugeilio'r Gwenith Gwyn
2   DYLAN THOMAS, WALES AND THE WELSH
3   Gwahoddiad
4   TO BEGIN AT THE BEGINNING, IN SWANSEA
5   Caersalem
6   DYLAN'S CARMARTHENSHIRE ROOTS
7   Ar Lan y Môr
8   NEW QUAY-AN INTERLUDE IN WEST WALES
9   Lausanne
10 OTHER PLACES
11 Mae'r Iesu yn Geidwad i Mi
12 LAUGHARNE - DYLAN'S RESTING PLACE Hen
Wlad fy Nhadau

CDs supplied by Fairplay Replication in West Wales
Fflach Records catalogue number CD337H 2012